Life, Liberty, Property & the Pursuit of Happiness

What it means to be an American

Life, Liberty, *Property* & the Pursuit of Happiness

What it means to be an American

Wesley B. Hoover

Cover design by Shannon Hoover

Published in the United States

First paperback edition published in 2012

To

Michele, my great and loyal wife, my soul mate

Alberta, my grand and noble mother, my inspiration

If you would not be forgotten
As soon as you are dead and rotten,
Either write things worthy reading,
Or do things worth the writing.

Benjamin Franklin

We hold these truths to be self-evident....

Thomas Jefferson

They that can give up essential liberty to obtain a little temporary safety deserve neither liberty nor safety...

Benjamin Franklin

Patrick Henry did *not* say, 'Give me absolute safety or give me death...
John Stossel

The greatest threat to mankind and civilization is the spread of the totalitarian philosophy. Its best ally is not the devotion of its followers but the confusion of its enemies. To fight it we must understand it.

Ayn Rand

Private property is the most important guarantee of freedom...

F. A. Hayek

In the end, more than they wanted freedom, they wanted security. They wanted a comfortable life, and they lost it all---security, comfort, and freedom. When...the freedom they wished for was freedom from responsibility, then Athens ceased to be free.....

Sir Edward Gibbon

To take from one because it is thought that his own industry and that of his father's has acquired too much, in order to spare to others, who, or whose fathers have not exercised equal industry and skill, is to violate arbitrarily the first principle of association---the guarantee to every one of a free exercise of his industry and the fruits acquired by it....

Thomas Jefferson

Men are that they might have Joy...

Table of Contents

SECTION FOUR - THE PURSUIT OF HAPPINESS

PREFACE

The making of America did not occur overnight nor in a decade around 1776. It was really begun in 1492 with the coming of Columbus, building with migration after migration until in the mid 1700's when nation-building became the focus of the majority of those living in this great land…The greatest land on God's green earth as Michael Medved loves to say, and a brand new country emerged. This new country ushered in the beginning of the greatest period of prosperity and freedom the world has ever known and perhaps will ever know. It truly was inspired and led by those we refer to as "The Founding Fathers". Educated men in histories, governments and politics, economics and philosophies they came from all walks of life, represented rich and poor alike, and were dedicated to creating a new and different structure and philosophy of government that had as its source of power and authority starting at the bottom with "the people" rather than from the top down as was and is the case with most countries and peoples throughout the world's history. It was known and criticized as "an experiment". It couldn't last in the face of population growth, world economic, social, and political pressures and would fail and succumb to being ruled by elites, landed, and the "blue-bloods" of history ruling the bulk of humanity as they have always done. That experiment continues, but not in the spirit nor letter as originally designed and intended. But I get ahead of myself.

In studying this country's origination, one is struck by the many brilliant one-liners that came from these men which for many became not only rallying cries to arms and defense, but to liberty and freedom themselves. Perhaps one of the greatest and

most-often quoted are the words penned by Thomas Jefferson himself which collectively became known as the Declaration of

Independence written in 1776. But before I get to that most famous one-liner, let me mention a few words of introduction.

For the most part the Declaration was a litany of grievances against King George and his "tyrannical" rule. But in the introductory paragraph we see not only its intent but the acknowledgement of God's laws and peoples' separate and equal station of entitlement to live under those laws;

> *"When in the Course of human events, it becomes necessary for one people to dissolve the political bands which have connected them with another, and to assume among the powers of the earth, the separate and equal station to which the Laws of Nature and of Nature's God entitle them, a decent respect to the opinions of mankind requires that they should declare the causes which impel them to the separation."*

These entitlements are further, clearly described in the paragraph which follows and here comes the famous one-liner:

> ***"We hold these truths to be self-evident, that all men are created equal, that they are endowed by their Creator with certain unalienable Rights, that among these are <u>Life, Liberty and the pursuit of Happiness.</u>—That to secure these rights, Governments are instituted among Men, deriving their just powers from the consent of the governed,--..."***

I have taken the liberty not only to write about the words of this most famous saying but to enlarge and add to their scope and breadth by including the concept of "Property" which I believe is most fundamental and deeply and inextricably connected to Life, Liberty and the Pursuit of Happiness in this mortal existence.

In the early days when America was in the making, slave-owners considered their slaves as "property" in the same vein as the holding of land, machinery, farm animals and so forth. To many this flew in the face of Jefferson's statement that

"...all men are created equal" endowed with rights to life and liberty and the pursuit of their own happiness. I believe that because of this dichotomy in the convictions of fellow countrymen, the "Fathers" scrupulously excluded the discussion of this principle, the rights of property, when structuring the initial principles on which this nation was founded. I further believe that the title of this book more clearly describes what this nation is all about in allowing all men the pursuit of their own happiness, and more importantly what it means to be an American.

FOREWORD

Our lives all intertwine in so many ways. First and foremost we need food and sustenance almost all of which involves others.

"Humans have a problem, and the problem is this: Food does not fall into their mouths. Even if it did, they would soon foul the place where they are lying. They could be burned by the sun, soaked by the rain, frozen by the wind. They could fall ill from disease, be plagued by insects, or be attacked by predators. They must find mates and reproduce. Their children must be cared for, or the children will also perish. And if even all this were done for humans, they would quickly succumb to boredom. To survive, they must take action.

"A man or woman, alone and naked, is all but helpless. Their actions are ineffectual. They lack the natural protection of fur or shell or hide. They lack the biological tools---claws, teeth, beaks, poison---with which to feed themselves. Even walking on a natural surface, without footwear, can be difficult. But the human has hands and a brain. With these two assets the human can create tools, discover techniques, and form organizations. In this way the human, born one of the weakest of all the creatures on Earth, has become the most powerful.

"Human beings are, from biological imperative, capitalists--- meaning only that they invest time and effort to create tools, techniques, and organizations to become more productive. Catching fish with the bare hands is possible, but not very efficient. To catch one fish, it may well be more efficient to use one's hands. To make a hook and line, a spear, or a net from naturally available materials takes time, effort, and technique, but humans calculate that the investment of time and effort will pay off in greater productivity in the future. They calculate, in

other words, that there will be a positive return on such a capital investment, that they will make a profit from their investment of effort, that their time is better spent making a hook and line than grasping at fish with their bare hands. By making a capital investment, humans expand their personal economy and productivity.

"Humans have a natural tendency to seek greater productivity, meaning only that they wish to act with greater effectiveness while using less time and effort...The term productivity, as used here, may have little relationship with official statistics. It does not matter what is wished for, whether more material goods, more services, more knowledge, more leisure, better interpersonal relationships, or even a more pristine natural environment, only that humans increase their ability to attain their wishes. The ends and means of production are limitless, but the urge to increase the ability to achieve those ends is inherent.

"A solitary human may as well be dead, since he or she will not reproduce alone. The human must find a mate and produce a child, thus engaging in cooperation with other humans.

"Unlike many species whose reproductive responsibilities are completed when they deposit their eggs or scatter their seeds, humans naturally form long-lasting families. In the basic family unit, humans not only invest their capital to make tools, but cooperate through the division of labor, specialization, and trade to improve their productivity still further. The wife is, by biological fact, responsible for the child's gestation, and is almost universally responsible for the child's care as an infant. The husband typically specializes in the production of food and shelter for the family. Although one rarely thinks of

transactions at such an intimate level as 'trade,' functionally it is no different than the trade that takes place between people living on different continents.

"Thus, even in their most simple state, humans can hardly exist without creating tools and building knowledge (capital investments), engaging in specialization and trade, jointly entering into productive endeavors (equity investment), and forming contracts, or promises, with others (bonds). The primary features of the modern capitalist market economy are apparent in the primitive family unit."

These words are taken from "Gold: The once and Future Money" by Nathan Lewis, Chapter one. Mortality, or life on this Earth very nearly falls into these descriptions no matter when or where humans live or lived. One can't even consume food nor find shelter without personal involvement as described above. No one is exempt if they still have a heartbeat.

OK, so here we are, mortal beings on a planet. Everyone generally is born with a will to live…to survive and also to thrive. Mostly, each one cares first about one's own surviving and thriving and thereafter to those near and dear. Given choices and opportunities each will step up and do the heavy lifting. All said actions are inherent in each one. Each person is equipped with complete entitlements or rights by nature and some say by design. The Founders said man is gifted with "Unalienable Rights"; meaning they are not granted by nor should be taken away by other men. They are inherent by nature, granted to man by God. Among these most precious and most important rights are 1) The Right to Life, 2) The Right to be Free and have Liberty, 3) The Rights of Property and Prosperity, and 4) The Right to Pursue Happiness and Joy as defined by each person.

Only a community or nation that lives by the rule of law can provide for the protection of man's rights consistently, correctly, and universally. The U. S. Constitution was designed for that purpose and I believe it is the very best system yet devised for the benefit of man, his community, his protection, and his mortal salvation. Would that we could live to deserve it and preserve it.

SECTION ONE
LIFE

"Life is sacred, that is to say, it is the supreme value which all other values are subordinate."   Albert Einstein

"You are not the momentary whim of a careless creator experimenting in the laboratory of life…You were made with a purpose."   Og Mandino

"Men are that they might have joy."   Jesus Christ

CHAPTER 1

EARTH LIFE

Life begins at forty is the popular saying. There is much truth to that when evaluating the quality of life. But the quality of life, at least in this writing, falls more into the last Section, The Pursuit of Happiness.

Life and Living is miraculous by nature. All matter in its basic form is lifeless and useless, that is to say without purpose. Life takes matter and puts it to use, usually with purpose. Life brings meaning to existence. We are….therefore.

The origin of Life is not known to the natural man. He can only observe what is; study what was and guess or theorize at how it all started. There is no observable, universal, empirical fact to prove life's origin or why life happens . We just know how to provide for it (by procreating, or the planting of seeds, etc.) and how it is destroyed. The natural man doesn't know why life exists or occurs.

But the truth of the matter is this; Life does exist on this planet. It will likely continue to exist, and it most definitely has purpose. Life, existence, is granted somehow. Someone or something causes it to happen. Why does matter suddenly take life, form, animate, move against gravity, develop and take on purpose, have a fixed existence then return to its previous, lifeless state? The natural man doesn't know why, he just knows that it does.

Evolution vs. Creationism

A primary difference between Evolution and Creationism in explaining how earth and all its inhabitants (both plant and animal) arrived in their present state is this; Evolution attempts to explain how the living came to be, and Creationism attempts to explain why.

To believe that the 'science' of Evolution is pure science takes an enormous leap of faith perhaps even more so than believing in a universal God. Asking us to accept as unquestionable facts the explanations of how earth was formed and how life originated and even how life changed to form different species when those 'facts' are admittedly offered as "theories" is simply ridiculous. And to declare these theories along with a mix of provable facts as evidence that there is no God does man an enormous injustice. So much of the doctrine of evolution involves purely pseudo-science as opposed to real science. That is fact. That is the truth. To claim that the doctrine of evolution proves that God does not exist is totally a lie, a sham, and a disgrace to human intelligence.

On the other hand, those believing that life got to be so as a result of an "Intelligent Design" and that by observing the mere complexity, beauty, the workings and uniqueness of the design provides proof that God does exist also requires an enormous leap of faith. At least the creationists acknowledge that belief in God does indeed require faith.

God did create the earth and all that is in and on it. What difference does it make how He did it or how long it took? What is most important to human beings, whether they know it or not, is why God did this. When humans come to understand this, they connect with God and thereafter, by further developing their faith, come to understand what God intends for each person. But I get ahead of myself.

Guess what? The real truth of the matter is that it is simply impossible to prove that God lives and created the Universe, or does not live and did not create the Universe using only empirical evidence or science, period. Both sides would do well to acknowledge this.

Both sides do have a place. Both deserve the right to be heard not only in society as a whole but in the classroom as well. Each serves real purpose. It is tragic that the evolutionist has persuaded society, through the legal process, to exclude the mention of God and His purpose in this nation's classrooms. Tragic because the moral connections to God and His purposes are being lost on society. There are no moral connections taught through evolution theory. America's children are being taught not to believe in God. Atheism is as much a "religion" as Christianity. If it is to be taught in classrooms, then the belief in God should also be taught. America should demand it, the people should fight for it, and they should change the system that prevents it, and by revolution if necessary.

Judeo-Christian Belief Structure Lies at the Core of America

The Founding Fathers, including Thomas Jefferson, when describing "Life" as an unalienable right of man granted by God, had in mind the God of Israel, without question. And the God of Israel said that He created all life on this planet.

"And God said, Let the earth bring forth grass, the herb yielding seed, and the fruit tree yielding fruit after his kind, whose seed is in itself, upon the earth; and it was so."

"And God said, Let the waters bring forth abundantly the moving creature that hath life, and fowl that may fly above the earth in the open firmament of heaven. And God created great whales, and every living creature that moveth, which the waters brought forth abundantly, after their kind, and every winged fowl after his kind..."

"And God made the beast of the earth after his kind, and cattle after their kind, and every thing that creepeth upon the earth after his kind..."

"And God said, Let us make man in our image, after our likeness: and let them have dominion over the fish of the sea, and over the fowl of the air, and over the cattle, and over all the earth, and over every creeping thing that creepeth upon the earth. So God created man in his own image, in the image of God created he him; male and female created he them."

That is the God that America was born and raised on. God granted life to all the earth and particularly to man. The Right to Life is granted by God and none other. Did everyone in America believe that, in the day of this nation's founding? Of course not, just like some do not believe even today. But enough did so then that it became a founding principle and still is at the core of America today. God lives and is the granter of all life. It matters not whether the majority or even one person believes it, to make it so. It does matter that the majority if not most do believe it, in order that it can continue to be taught to all men. Let each succeeding generation thereafter decide for itself to believe or not to believe after having been so taught.

Earth was Created for the Benefit of Man

Thomas Paine said it well when he wrote, *"It is wrong to say that God made the rich and the poor; He made only male and female, and He gave them the whole earth for their inheritance."* Even God said,

"Behold, I have given you (man) every herb bearing seed, which is upon the face of all the earth, and every tree, in the which is the fruit of a tree yielding seed; to you it shall be for meat....And every beast of the earth, and every fowl of the air, and every thing that creepeth upon the earth, wherein there is life..."

"So God created man in his own image, in the image of God created he him; male and female created he them. And God blessed them, and God said unto them, Be fruitful, and multiply, and replenish the earth, and subdue it: and have dominion over the fish of the sea, and over the fowl of the air, and over every living thing that moveth upon the earth."

Man is higher than the Animals

Animals do not have rights in the same way and to the extent that man has. They exist only to serve and bless man. They have no higher purpose than that for which they were created. That they deserve to remain on earth and be protected from man-caused extinction goes without question. For God commanded that man should replenish the earth. He is not entitled to commit wanton destruction and to be irresponsible in his dominion. But he is entitled to kill, eat, and otherwise consume animals for what they can provide. Animals are to be used for the benefit of man, period. Should they be treated humanely? Yes, but that doesn't mean they cannot be killed and consumed in order to fulfill their purpose on earth. Do they have rights over man as to where they can live? Absolutely not!

Human, Mortal Life is Sacred

That God created man and gave him life and dominion is reason enough to conclude that mortal, human life is sacred. God intended that man should have not only a mortal existence but an immortal, eternal destiny. In that vein, life takes on supreme even more sacred meaning and purpose. When in the 10 Commandments, God instructed that "Thou shalt not Kill" He meant not killing another human being in an act of aggression, dominion over, or to take the right of life away from another without just cause (as in defense of Freedom, family, or self protection). Human life.....is indeed, sacred.

CHAPTER 2

———◈———

WHEN DOES
MORTAL LIFE BEGIN

Every scientist or student of human biology knows that a new entity has been created at the instant of conception like unto a seed as it were, and that a new life begins the instant that the new entity attaches itself to the mother's womb. There just is no debate on that fact. Conception is nothing less than a miracle of miracles, so incredibly complex in its scope yet so simple in its reality. Two separate, simple, microscopically viable cells coming together to form a new entity. An entity that is absolutely separate and distinct from either of its two parents. Living matter that has every physical characteristic instantly genetically stamped into its very existence, defining innumerable features so different from every other living human being, revealed by fingerprints and DNA to name a few; so many and different that absolutely no two human beings are exactly alike.

To exist, develop and grow that new life requires constant nurturing provided by its mother. The nurturing of life continues through gestation, birth, developing into adulthood in stages, each of which has purpose and value. Life, throughout these various stages, can and does end from natural causes.

The Sanctity of Life has been drastically Compromised
Sometime in the middle of the 20th century, the debate has arisen trying to define when life becomes "viable" such that it can be protected by laws and rights. The debate has been enlarged (and clouded) to include whether a woman, bearing a child, has certain rights over her body that trump the rights of that separate life within her. Everyone reading this well knows

that debate or debates. Anyone supporting "a woman's right of choice" has either not understood the sanctity of life or has chosen to ignore it. The argument, distorted as it has become, that the woman's choice is over her own body, so clearly avoids the truth of the matter, as to become nonsensical by its very argument. The real choice that women have, which not only is clearly correct but fair, is whether to have unprotected sex or not, plain and simple. That is clearly their free right of choice, a choice which may or may not render them pregnant with an unwanted child. If they have chosen to participate in the act of procreation without adequate protection, and they then become pregnant, then they should not and clearly do not have the inherent right to destroy (or have destroyed) that life which is living separately and distinctly within the woman's body.

What about rape, incest, etc.? Let's not even go there as those arguments can be solved fairly and justly in favor of a woman who is truly victim. And besides, the number of such cases is so miniscule compared to the cases of women who willingly made the choice to put themselves in the situations that they did. The vast preponderance of all abortion cases applies to the phony, and "politically correct right of choice". At-will abortion has tragically become a prophylactic of choice.

As one might expect, once the body of public thought arrived to the point where abortion was to become nothing more than an acceptable form of birth control, there arose an onslaught of effort to create a "legal" right to do so, to give credence to such a vile and reprehensible practice. Said right was conveniently provided for by one of the most grievous legal travesties to occur in the history of America.

Roe v. Wade
Roe v. Wade, a landmark case of the US Supreme Court, is one of the most controversial and politically significant cases in US Supreme Court history, greatly affecting political elections and

decisions ever since. In essence, the decision held that a mother may abort her pregnancy for any reason, up until the "point at which the fetus becomes viable." The court defined viable as being "potentially able to live outside the mother's womb, albeit with artificial aid," adding that viability "is usually placed at about seven months..." The court rested its decision almost entirely on the basis of the "right of privacy" clause found in the 14th Amendment. Justice Harry Blackmun in writing the majority view, said, "that there was no legal grounds for ...any right to life of the unborn fetus. The fetus would have such a right if it were defined as a legal person for purposes of the Fourteenth Amendment, but the original intent of the Constitution...did not include protection of the unborn." Where Mr. Blackmun came to that conclusion is beyond human understanding.

Most constitutionalists have concluded the argument was formulated out of "thin air" finding absolutely no basis from the Constitution, particularly the 14th amendment, to conclude a right of abortion whatsoever.

Every aspect of this court decision was faulty---the constitutional arguments, the biological arguments, and the historical arguments---as even many proponents of abortion rights acknowledge. It is bad constitutional law; or rather it is not constitutional law at all and gives almost no sense of an obligation to try to be.

Both the existence of life and the right to life are granted by God and are unalienable. They are not rights granted by man or to be taken away by man. Roe v. Wade can and must be overturned. This travesty must be corrected.

Mortal Life is not the Beginning of Life
Anyone who ponders life for any length of time has surely wondered as to the "why" of it. Why does God do this, grant

life that is? "Why am I here"? More on this is discussed in Chapter 3. "Where did I come from?" is another question which often arises when reflecting on the miracle of life.

The Church of Jesus Christ of Latter-Day-Saints (the Mormons) has a very distinct belief structure, regarding the existence and purpose of life, different from almost all of their fellow counter-parts in the Christian World (collectively known as Catholic and Protestant). Some of those distinctions involve the belief regarding individual life, its origin and destiny.

Their doctrine holds that man existed in a pre-mortal, spirit life, an existence created by God preparatory to coming to this mortal state. Men are literally (not figuratively) children of God, spiritually, that is to say in spirit form.

Here is a short list of scriptural references documenting man's pre-mortal life:

1. *"God of the spirits of all flesh" Num. 16:22*
2. *"Ye are the children of the Lord your God" Deut. 14:1*
3. *"..there is a spirit in man" Job 32:8*
4. *"..the spirit shall return unto God who gave it" Eccl. 12:7*
5. *"..we are the offspring of God" Acts 17:29*
6. *"..spirits...taken home to that God who gave them life" Alma 40:11*
7. *"..inhabitants thereof are begotten sons and daughters of God" D&C 76:24*
8. *"I made the world, and men before they were in the flesh" Moses 6:51*
9. *"..in heaven created I them, and there was not yet flesh upon the earth" Moses 3:5*
10. *"..spirit and the body are the soul of man" D&C 88:15*

When does man's spirit enter into his mortal body?

Life

We know that mortal life begins at the instant of conception when the male sperm unites with the female egg and that new entity attaches itself to the mother's body. That is a new life, separate and distinct from its mother in whom it will be nurtured until birth. It is alive and growing.

The spirit is what gives life to man. The spirit gives life and movement to inanimate objects or matter. There can be no living matter that does not contain a spirit since it is the spirit that gives life to the inanimate. Mortal life cannot exist without a living spirit. Without a spirit, no life can exist. No matter how you say it, the spirit of man enters in when that new life begins growing within the mother's body. And that is the truth.

Life

CHAPTER 3

———————— ◉ ————————

WHERE DID I COME FROM?
Why am I Here?

"Our birth...Hath had elsewhere its setting...And cometh from afar... trailing clouds of glory, do we come   From God, who is our home"
William Wordsworth

Man's Pre-mortal Existence Helps Explain the Purpose of Mortal Life

No matter how long man studies the universe he cannot by his own, come to know why he exists merely by that study. Is there some purpose to all this life? What is or was God's intent in creating life? Am I left on my own to find life's meaning?

All men are literal sons and daughters of God. We are his offspring. We are his spirit children, every one. We existed as such with God before this earth was created. And that is why all men were created equal, because we all have emanated from Him.

Here is another short list of scriptures that refer to the nature of man's pre-mortal life and the purpose of life:

1. *"Before I formed thee in the belly I knew thee; and before thou camest forth out of the womb I sanctified thee, and I ordained thee a prophet unto the nations."* Jer. 1:5

2. *"..chosen us in him before the foundation of the world"* Eph. 1:4

3. *"That by him, and through him, and of him, the worlds are and were created, and the inhabitants thereof are begotten sons and daughters unto God."* D&C 76:24

13

4. "..called and prepared from the foundation of the world" Alma 13:3

5. "..before they were born.. received their first lessons" D&C 138:56

6. "And thus God bringeth about his great and eternal purposes, which were prepared from the foundation of the world..." Alma 43:26

7. "..for mine own purpose have I made these things" Moses 1:31

8. "For behold, this is my work and my glory, to bring to pass the immortality and eternal life of man" Moses 1:39

In this pre-mortal existence, man was endowed with agency or individual choice. Four great principles must be in force concomitant to agency: 1) Laws must exist; laws ordained by an Omnipotent power; laws which can be obeyed or disobeyed. 2) Opposites must exist---good and evil, virtue and vice, right and wrong---that is, there must be an opposition, one force pulling one way and another pulling the other. 3) A knowledge of good and evil must be had by those who are to enjoy the agency, that is, they must know the difference between the opposites. 4) An unfettered power of choice must prevail.

It is God's work and his glory to bring to pass the immortality and eternal life of man. An eternal plan to accomplish this was laid out to all men in their pre-mortal life, and having been endowed with agency, the power of choice, all men arriving on earth in this mortal state, chose to come and partake in this opportunity and they did so without coercion of any kind.

"Endowed with agency and subject to eternal laws, man began his progression and advancement in pre-mortal existence, his ultimate goal being to attain a state of glory, honor, and exaltation like the Father of spirits. During his earth life he gains a mortal body, receives experience in earthly things, and

Life

prepares for a future eternity after the resurrection when he will continue to gain knowledge and intelligence. This gradual unfolding course of advancement and experience---a course that began in a past eternity and will continue in ages future--- is frequently referred to as a course of eternal progression."

Bruce R. McConkie

Life

CHAPTER 4

——◉——

WHY BAD THINGS HAPPEN
IN THIS LIFE

How can a Loving Heavenly Father allow Bad Things to Happen?

It is not enough just to say 'all things happen for a reason', 'God's purposes are unknown to man', or 'we don't know why we just accept', etc. No wonder many conclude this is blind faith or that if God ever existed He is now dead, because it stands to reason that if God loved and cared about man, He would not, could not let bad things happen. And since bad things do happen, therefore there cannot be a God.

Generally, all bad things that happen to man can be lumped into two categories; One, natural events commonly (and probably erroneously) referred to as "acts of God". Things like hurricanes, tornadoes, earthquakes, trees blowing over onto innocent children, devastating floods, etc., would fall into this category. Two, acts of man against man such as holocausts, murder, theft, wanton destruction and oppression (the list is endless); all seem unfair to the unwary, innocent victim and bystander.

Death and suffering happens. It was by design that this is so. There is no greater time that man most contemplates God as when he is facing crisis. As the saying goes, "There are no atheists in foxholes."

But, the question bears reason; why does God allow these things to happen? Can He, should He intervene to protect those deserving and/or pleading for his help?

God (and the Earth) obeys Natural Laws

Gravity and the Earth's magnetism are natural laws. In organizing and assembling this universe, God obeyed natural law. All matter has existed from eternity; it was not created out of nothing. The earth obeys and is acted upon by natural laws, revolving around the sun as it does, and all else that occurs on, in or above the earth does so in the natural course of things. It is what it is.

WHY GOD CANNOT, DOES NOT INTERVENE

The fact that God cannot, does not intervene can only be discovered by understanding what happened in our pre-mortal existence. An understanding which includes knowing why God created this earth for man in the first place.

The Law of Eternal Progression

Man set upon the course of eternal progression in becoming spirit sons and daughters of God in our pre-mortal life. In that state man did not have all the desirable attributes of God; did not, could not have all attributes God would like his children to have. God wants all his children to have all (attributes and more) of what He is and has. To progress to that point required mans' obtaining an immortal (that is to say, resurrected) body of flesh and bone, and developing godlike attributes both of which could only be obtained by coming to the earth and living outside God's presence. God's purpose and plan is best described by his own words: *"For behold, this is my work and my glory to bring to pass the immortality and eternal life of man."*

Earth-life is not an end in and of itself. But it is a necessary step in the progress of man. It is a precursor, a preparatory state to the post-mortal life or existence which God has prepared for his children.

The Free Agency of Man

18

God's plan for his children is referred to as "The Plan of Salvation". In order to obtain all the attributes God wishes for His children, the plan requires that man come to a mortal state of existence to not only obtain this mortal body, but to see if man could abide by and be obedient to God's laws outside of God's presence. Man must live by faith using his free agency and if science could empirically prove that God existed, the plan of salvation would be completely thwarted and this life would cease to be the testing ground for which it was designed.

Man is not a play toy of God or the gods. God does not tinker, experiment, intervene, or control man in any way against man's will. He cannot for a very specific reason. God has granted unto His children, this free agency. Man is free to choose…has freedom of choice and it existed in the pre-existence.

In laying out the plan to His children in the pre-existence, God made it clear that this life, this mortal, natural state of being, involved what it involves. In other words, we completely understood that natural laws could result in "disasters" of all kinds, but we made the choice to come here anyway, in spite of these dangers because we wanted to not only experience the joys of earth-life and yes grow from its challenges, but we also willingly accepted the challenges it would present to see if we could meet the tests and achieve the rewards that God intended for us to achieve. So we decided to embark on the journey called God's Plan of Salvation which has so much more meaning beyond this earthly mortal existence.

Death, pain, suffering, trials and tribulations are inherent in this earthly, mortal existence. We knew beforehand that mortal life would have these circumstances and conditions, yet we still chose to come anyway. But we also knew that earth-life would be filled with good things too; beauty, love, enlightenment, joy and happiness as well. But because earth-life is not an end in and of itself, man's mortal life pales in comparison to his spiritual life which has the most bearing upon man's eternal happiness. But again, I get ahead of myself.

Why God allows evil to exist

Okay, but what about evil in the world. Why does God allow that to happen? Isn't it enough that man must endure pain and suffering caused by natural conditions and circumstances?

In answering that question, one must also refer to the answer to the question: "Why am I here?" Here again we go back to our pre-mortal existence. It is God's intent, indeed his "work and glory", for us to have "…all that He is and has"; to have all His attributes, glories, and joys. However, most if not all those things, God cannot just implant into His children. They must be developed, gained and realized through man's own efforts. God can teach, lead, encourage and establish laws but He can neither grant godlike attributes nor can He force man to obtain them. Man, only by using his agency and being obedient can he obtain Godlike attributes from his own experiences, challenges, and trials. And to do that man must be on his own, to live by faith and faith alone. Man must live by faith outside of God's presence and that is achieved in this, man's mortal, earthly existence. And that is why we are here, at least one of the reasons. And that is also why God does not readily reveal Himself, nor can His reality be empirically proven, nor can He intervene to force good and prevent evil on earth. To do so would destroy man's agency, eliminate the purpose of mortal life, lay waste all God's creations, and defeat His 'work and glory'.

Man is granted his free agency, or rather his agency is free and it is universal. He is free to commit mayhem if he chooses or to do good. He can either choose to believe in God or not to believe and he can act accordingly. And that is the truth.

The Universality of the Belief in God

Not that numbers or percentages matter, because it doesn't figure in that because a certain number of people believe something, that that is therefore so. The following is not offered as any sort of proof, just that it is and always has been so. And that is the universality of the belief in God. Read any history of any people who ever lived on earth and it will be found that all generations believe in the existence of God. Whether that belief translates into pure good and righteous living is another matter, not to be treated here. But the fact remains that all men, eventually, believe. Oh sure, elitists, philosophers, logical thinkers in great numbers can point to their reasoning as proof that He doesn't, cannot exist.

Things like, "Can God create a rock (if he is omnipotent) greater than he can lift?" "Did God really create the earth in 7 days (seven twenty-four hour periods)?" are typical questions of logic, which help the elitists foster their agnosticism and atheism. But those, if they really do so believe, are but a mere drop in the ocean of those who definitely believe that God lives and is connected to them in some infinite way.

This universal connection to God, or belief in God, is also manifested in the belief that life continues to exist beyond the grave. Death does not permanently destroy all that lives. You would be hard-pressed to find more than a pittance, the number of people who ever believed that. Life, after we die continues to exist.

Well now, we have addressed, in the context of LIFE, 1) Who we (mankind) are, 2) Where we came from, 3) Why we are here. But the question of where we are going is yet another often-pondered query of life.

Where are we going?

Life

The question of where we are going after this life will not be addressed in this work, except to stress that there is a life hereafter. The focus of this book is on this the mortal, earth life. God prepared this earth, we agreed to come here in pursuit of great lofty purpose, and we are here blessed with life and living; an unalienable right granted to us by God himself. That is fact and it is the truth. We are free to chose whether to believe it nor not. Take the time to contemplate it.

CHAPTER 5

---●---

BELIEVING IN GOD

How Many Believe in God, The Grantor of Life?

It is both correct and logical to deal with the question of the existence of God when contemplating this miracle of life, this concept recognized by the country's founders as both a gift from God and a right granted by him. There cannot be one without the other. God and life are inseparably connected and when men contemplate life they automatically think of God. One has to work against his inner being to conclude that God does not exist. He has to exert great effort to draw away and even then, men still believe, in the final analysis. Again, as the saying goes, there are no atheists in foxholes. When faced with the prospect of death, it is absolutely universal that all men contemplate God and their relationship with that holy being.

Logic, on the one hand, is (ostensibly) the science of correct reasoning; a science which deals with the criteria of valid thought. It is the necessary connection or outcome, as through the working of cause and effect. Logic, however, is the course of thinking that both the evolutionist and the true believer in God use to defend their positions against each other; concepts which are diabolically opposed to one another.

The evolutionist, through science and the study of natural selection or survival of the fittest, mutational theory, and speciation or how species evolve; through these concepts show that the world of the living has evolved over millions of years. This proves that the world and all living upon it was not created in seven 24-hour periods as the Bible would have us believe. And since the Bible is the basis of Judeo-Christian core of beliefs, then to believe in God as the world's creator is folly indeed.

The Judeo-Christian believer counters that the creation of earth and life upon it was completed in 6 periods, metaphorically referred to as "days", with the Lord "resting from his labors" on the seventh "day". And that the real message in this doctrine is not how God did the creation or how long it took, but that he rested from all his labors (of the 6 previous periods) on the Sabbath or seventh day. God has commanded that men rest from all earthly work and cares, one day out of seven, yes even to keep it holy to contemplate and worship God, visit the sick, etc; a commandment that even He himself kept when creating the universe. And further, the believer points to all the wondrous beauty of life and earth, its vast complexities, so vast that more is discovered every day, and the intricacies of the universe and how it all works together seemingly following a most complex and grand design; all this points to a great "designer" as it simply could not have been created from nothing nor come to existence merely by chance. Evolutionary theoretical reasoning does not explain or fulfill the empirical reality.

So logic, when put to test, can lead to diabolically diverse conclusions. Logic can be at fault or it can lead to truth. But logic is not the basis whereby all men believe in God. Before dealing further in depth with that concept, we should consider the universality of belief beforehand. We should show the universality first before discussing how it is that all men believe.

The Universality of the Belief in God

There is no recorded history of mankind where a society of people ever existed that did not believe in the existence of God. It simply cannot be found. Even paganism had a God of all Gods. This reality is virtually universal and is indisputable. Every recorded history testifies that this is and was so. The influence of this universal belief figures in all societal relationships as they emerge and exist.

That there are groups of supposed non-believers and doubters, who through their applied logic scenarios conclude God does not exist, or God did exist but is now dead, or God may or may not exist; there can be no doubt. Men can draw away from or forget God at times in their lives; they can rebel and fight against God; and they can replace God in their lives with gods of other persuasions such as money, power, fame and the like. But in the final analysis, when fear, tragedy, severe loss, deep uncertainty, and/or acute adversity inevitably emerge, men naturally, even universally, turn to God and appeal to His influence, mercy, forgiveness, and spiritual sustenance. And therein exists one of the purposes in this mortal life and the ever present vicissitudes which beset mankind. Without the risks presented in mortal life such as natural tragedies and evils which occur, men perhaps would have no need or ever be persuaded to believe in and appeal to God at all.

Liberty

CHAPTER 6

———————○○———————

WHY ALL MEN BELIEVE IN GOD

One of the many definitions given in any typical dictionary of the word "light" is this; knowledge, enlightenment, mental illumination. This feature of truth is given by God when He Himself describes the universality of all men believing in Him. And there is a profound connection between this "light" and "life" as we shall see by pondering the words of God and Jesus Christ.

God, through His own words and also through the words of Christ, has declared how it is that all men know and believe in Him, and it has to do with these two concepts; light and life. He has given it a name…"The Light of Christ". Consider his words as follows:

"He that ascended up on high, as also He descended below all things, in that He comprehended all things, that He might be in all and through all things, the 'light of truth;

"Which truth shineth. This is the light of Christ. As also He is in the sun, and the light of the sun, and the power thereof by which it was made.

"As also He is in the moon, and is the light of the moon, and the power thereof by which it was made;

"As also the light of the stars, and the power thereof by which they were made;

"And the earth also, and the power thereof, even the earth upon which you stand.

"And the light which shineth, which giveth you light, is through Him who enlighteneth your eyes, which is the same light that quickeneth your understandings;

"Which light proceedeth forth from the presence of God to fill the immensity of space—

"The light which is in all things, which giveth life to all things, which is the law by which all things are governed, even the power of God who sitteth upon his throne, who is in the bosom of eternity, who is in the midst of all things."

God has also instructed that man should live by every word that proceeds forth from Him and in doing so He reveals again this universality of light given to all men.

"For you shall live by every word that proceedeth forth from the mouth of God.

"For the word of the Lord is truth, and whatsoever is truth is light, and whatsoever is light is Spirit, even the Spirit of Jesus Christ.

"And the Spirit giveth light to every man that cometh into the world; and the Spirit enlighteneth every man through the world...."

Here are further words of an ancient prophet:

"For behold, the Spirit of Christ is given to every man, that he may know good from evil; wherefore, I show unto you the way to judge; for every thing which inviteth to do good, and to persuade to believe in Christ (or God), is sent forth by the power and gift of Christ; wherefore ye may know with a perfect knowledge it is of God."

It is because of the light of Christ that all men know good from evil and enjoy the guidance of what is sometimes commonly called *conscience.* It is the Spirit by means of which God is omnipresent; it is the light which enables Christ to be in all things, and through all things, and round about all things. It gives life to all things, is the law by which they are governed, and the power of God is manifest through it.

So that is how all men know there is a God of the universe. All life, light and truth emanate from Him through Christ. All men believe. Whether they adhere to the light of Christ is another matter, however.

Liberty

CHAPTER 7

———————●———————

LIFE IS A TEST

Life, the right to life, the light of Christ are all gifts of God to man. Men also are given the gift of agency, the power and right to choose, as previously mentioned. God gives commandments and instructions as to how to live (and for reason and purpose), but He does not force men to be obedient, for that would defeat the purpose of mortality and God's plan for His children. Nor are men destined or predestined to do either good or evil. They have choice and agency and can totally believe and act accordingly. God does not have a plan for you whereby you are forced or destined to follow. Agency is universal and is the controlling factor in all matters of behavior and belief.

It is fact that all men are given the power to know God lives, and the power to know right from wrong, evil and good. It naturally follows therefore, that all men know that the purpose of life is to test us and see if we will adhere to the spirit given within us.

As man becomes further enlightened as to God's will for His children by absorbing His word as it has been revealed through His prophets from the beginning even to this present day, the tests presented become even more acute and significant. But along with those tests come a better understanding of God, His nature, His plan for His children, as well as a fuller, richer, more fulfilling life, a life full of purpose, joy and great happiness.

Life, therefore, as envisioned by the Founding Fathers was significant as to be mentioned first when enumerating the rights of man. But life is even more than a miracle, embodied with significant rights. It is sacred, hallowed and blessed by God

Himself. The connection between the lives of men and God is so profound that it is beyond the scope of human understanding. Not only are we His literal children but the connections that are made possible by and through the atonement of His son can expand to the point that eventually man can have all that God has, even to become as He is and have all that He has, if man can be obedient to the pattern of living laid down by God Himself. That course of living can only be obtained or revealed, or developed on earth by and through God's chosen leaders holding the power and authority granted by Him, and by people adhering to those teachings.

But our intent in this writing is to dwell on the miracle, blessing, beauty and rights of life. I love these words of President Ronald Reagan all of which form the entire epitaph on his tombstone as follows:

> *"I know in my heart that man is good;*
> *That what is right will always eventually triumph;*
> *And there is purpose and worth to each and every life."*

I second that.

SECTION 2

LIBERTY

"What is it that gentlemen wish? What would they have? Is life so dear, or peace so sweet, as to be purchased at the price of chains and slavery? Forbid it, Almighty God! I know not what course others may take; but as for me, **_give me liberty or give me death!_** *"*　　　　　Patrick Henry, March 23, 1775.

"Concentrated power is not rendered harmless by the good intentions of those who create it."　　　　Milton Friedman

"Liberty means responsibility. That is why most men dread it."
George Bernard Shaw

"As long as human beings are imperfect, there will always be arguments for extending the power of government to deal with these imperfections. The only logical stopping place is totalitarianism—unless we realize that tolerating imperfections is the price of freedom."　　　　Dr. Thomas Sowell

A man and a woman draw together and form a relationship, which if they intend for it to endure time, they enlarge that relationship to form a bond or contract. When children come along, a family is born. Families grow into tribes. Tribes grow into communities and communities grow into states and nations. At every level and in every instance, all individuals are faced with the same basic tasks of providing for their food, shelter, safety and protection, and the need to provide solutions to all life's problems, challenges and disagreements.

Life is a struggle. Almost nothing except breath and life is totally universal. And as societies develop and grow, the question of how the needs of all can be accomplished is at the heart of all human existence. How shall the land and seas and all their resources be divided? Who will provide protection for all? Who will lead, how or why?

For the most part, no one is born into a two parent family, into a world where no one else lives, and into a world where there is total freedom to choose how to accomplish all of that individual's needs and desires. Except in rare cases where families, groups or tribes migrate into uninhabited areas, where new associations, rules, etc. are forged, everyone is born to already existing societal establishments. And yet, no matter what type of society is established into which one is born, each individual is still faced with the same basic tasks of providing food, shelter, etc.

CHAPTER 1

━━━●━━━

UNIVERSAL YEARNING
TO BE FREE

Men are not born into nor do they naturally migrate into an amorphous state or body without separate identity. No civilization of any size, in any age has been so characterized. Water can be segregated into many drops or evaporated into the air, but when it comes together again, no one drop or molecule is readily distinguishable from another. Not so with mankind. No two people can be said to have exactly the same characteristics, exactly the same tastes, desires, aspirations or anything; except perhaps one thing....the universal desire to be free. To have the freedom of choice: To come and go when we please; to eat what we want; to purchase what we want and can afford, when we want it; to associate with whom we want; believe in what we want to believe in; speak what we want to speak; these and more are desired freedoms that are universal. And that fact is simply undeniable. To argue otherwise is folly and without merit.

Men yearn to be free. So, are all men free? Of course not, but they still yearn to be. Do they tolerate the lack of freedoms? Yes, for all kinds of reasons. But that they yearn to be free is inherent by nature because man is endowed with his own agency which is a gift granted unto man by God. A man convinced against his will, is of the same opinion still; as the saying goes. The will and conscience dictate. And the will and conscience as endowed by God are inherently free, and that is the truth.

Agency, will and conscience are often viewed as the same thing. And freedom is an inseparable partner. This is recognized by many great thinkers. Consider these words of a man named Mikhail A. Bakunin:

"Freedom is the absolute right of all adult men and women to seek permission for their action only from their own conscience and reason, and to be determined in their actions only by their will, and consequently to be responsible only to themselves, and then to the society to which they belong, but only insofar as they have made a free decision to belong to it."

And these words from Marcus Tullius Cicero: *"Freedom is the power to live as you will."*

I believe Herbert Hoover recognized that free agency was inherent when he spoke these words:

"Freedom is a thing of the spirit. Men must be free to worship, to think, to hold opinions, to speak without fear. They must be free to challenge wrong and oppression with surety of justice. Freedom conceives that the mind and spirit of man can be free only if he be free to pattern his own life, to develop his own talents, free to earn, to spend, to save, to acquire property as the security of his old age and his family."

Poetry speaks truths in pleasing phrases with words that stir our souls and enlighten our understandings. These poetic words are taken from an LDS church hymn and speak of the universality of freedom's yearning:

Know then that ev'ry soul is free,
To choose his life and what he'll be;
For this eternal truth is given,
That God will force no man to heaven.

He'll call, persuade direct him right;,
Bless him with wisdom, love, and light;

Liberty

In nameless ways be good and kind;
But never force the human mind.

Freedom and reason make us men:
Take these away, what are we then?
Mere animals, and just as well,
The beasts may think of heaven or hell.

May we no more our powers abuse,
But ways of truth and goodness choose;
Our God is pleased when we improve
His grace, and seek His perfect love.

It's my free will for to believe:
'Tis God's free will me to receive:
To stubborn willers this I'll tell,
It's all free grace, and all free will.

Those that despise, grow harder still;
Those that adhere, he turns their will:
And thus despisers sink to hell,
While those that hear in glory dwell.

But if we take the downward road,
And make in hell our last abode;
Our God is clear, and we shall know,
We've plunged ourselves in endless wo.

Liberty

CHAPTER 2

———•———

WHAT FREEDOM IS NOT

A society that puts equality...ahead of freedom will end up with
neither...:   Milton Friedman

Individual freedom is explained in chapter 1. Individual freedom is man's free agency. It is universal and God-given. Societal freedom is another matter altogether. Here even the definitions as to what freedom is vary as colors vary and contrast as night differs from day. There just is no universal definition of freedom that explains what everyone means when setting forth any sort of understanding to the word. Or perhaps more correctly said, everyone understands what the word means, but putting the meaning into practice is where mass misunderstandings and vast abuses arise.

One would think that with an all-inclusive, all-encompassing notion or yearning to be free, that the end result would almost always gravitate towards universal freedom to the masses. But sadly, in almost the entire history of mankind, the exact opposite has been the actual result. Except only in very rare instances in recorded history has there ever been any sort of societal freedom to the masses. Instead, the vast majority of people who have ever lived on this planet including to this present day, have lived under tyrannical rule and have been governed or dictated to from the top down, rather than be governed from the bottom up.

In perhaps one of the greatest hoaxes ever perpetrated upon man, Karl Marx who lived in the early 20th century in Germany, wrote along with his colleague, Friedrich Engels, *The Communist Manifesto.*

Marx's theories about society, economics and politics, which are collectively known as Marxism, hold that all societies progress through the dialectic of class struggle. He was heavily critical of the predominant socio-economic form of society, capitalism, which he called the "dictatorship of the bourgeoisie", believing it to be run by the wealthy middle and upper classes purely for their own benefit, and predicted that, like previous socioeconomic systems, it would inevitably produce internal tensions which would lead to its self-destruction and replacement by a new system, socialism. Under socialism, he argued, society would be governed by the working class in what he called the "dictatorship of the proletariat", the "workers state" or "workers' democracy". He believed that socialism would, in its turn, eventually be replaced by a stateless, classless society called pure communism. Along with believing in the inevitability of socialism and communism, Marx actively fought for the former's implementation, arguing that both social theorists and underprivileged people should carry out organized revolutionary action to topple capitalism and bring about socio-economic change.

History has shown what actually resulted from this unnatural nonsense. With the rise of V. I. Lenin, Joseph Stalin, Chairman Mao, Pol Pot, and many others, the masses being deluded into believing that their ultimate freedom would be the result of their blind adherence to this pack of lies, instead have been enslaved to the greatest extent and have been forced into living under the most repressive dictatorships in all history.

As mentioned, almost all people who have ever lived on the planet have lived under one form of dictatorship or another, at least until the rise of Republicanism and the miracle of America. Rulers of all kinds, calling themselves Aghas, Caesars, Chancellors, Chiefs, Duces, Dukes, Emperors, Fuhrers, Imams, Incas, Kaisers, Kings, Lords, Magistrates,

Monarchs, Nobles, Pharaohs, Priests, Princes, Shahs, Sheikhs, Sultans, and Tsars, Premiers, Prime Ministers, and yes even Presidents, to name only a few, have held sway over the masses, almost all of which against the will of the people. People considered to be of elevated rank have been in control through centralized power and consolidation.

Such control over the governed has been almost entirely gained by either military force or by massive propagandistic methods or both. Kingdoms conquering Kingdoms, Provinces controlling Provinces, etc. make up the histories of the world. It was the norm, it was the reality of existence.

Violence and force have been the most obvious method of controlling populations. But perhaps the use of propaganda has been the most pervasive and persuasive.

Propaganda

"Most people prefer to believe that their leaders are just and fair, even in the face of evidence to the contrary, because once a citizen acknowledges that the government under which he lives is lying and corrupt, the citizen has to choose what he or she will do about it. To take action in the face of corrupt government entails risks of harm to life and loved ones. To choose to do nothing is to surrender one's self-image of standing for principles. Most people do not have the courage to face that choice. Hence, most propaganda is not designed to fool the critical thinker but only to give moral cowards an excuse not to think at all."   Michael Rivero

Propaganda is necessary to foster tolerance of dictatorships. There is probably no better example of that than in Hitler's Nazi Germany which enabled him to rise to power as a mighty dictator, through violent means and to be accepted, practically worshipped, as the venerable "Das Fuhrer".

Joseph Goebbels was the author of perhaps the greatest propaganda machinery ever devised. He was the great facilitator leading the way for Hitler's rise to power. As Reichsminister for Propaganda and National Enlightenment, Goebbels was given complete control over radio, press, cinema, and theater; later he also regimented all German culture. Goebbels placed his undeniable intelligence and his brilliant insight into mass psychology entirely at the service of his party. His most virulent propaganda was against the Jews. As a hypnotic orator he was second only to Hitler, and in his staging of mass meetings and parades he was unsurpassed. Utterly cynical, he seems to have believed only in the self-justification of power. He remained loyal to Hitler until the very end. On May 1, 1945, as Soviet troops were storming Berlin, Goebbels committed suicide.

Goebbels' (and perhaps all dictators') Principles of Propaganda

Here is a short list of these principals as prepared and defined by Goebbels himself. See if you don't recognize any connections or familiarity to the arguments being used today for strong, centralized governmental power:

1. The Propagandist must have access to intelligence concerning events and public opinion.
2. Propaganda must be planned and executed by only one authority.
3. Propaganda requires that there be an "enemy or enemies".
4. Propaganda must affect the enemy's policy and action.
   a. By suppressing propagandistically desirable material which can provide the enemy with useful intelligence.
   b. By openly disseminating propaganda whose content or tone causes the enemy to draw the desired conclusions.

    c. By goading the enemy into revealing vital information about himself.

    d. By making no reference to a desired enemy activity when any reference would discredit that activity.

5. To be perceived, propaganda must evoke the interest of an audience and must be transmitted through an attention-getting communications medium.

6. Credibility alone must determine whether propaganda output should be true or false.

7. The purpose, content and effectiveness of "enemy" propaganda; the strength and effects of an expose; and the nature of current propaganda campaigns determine whether enemy propaganda should be ignored or refuted.

8. Propaganda must be carefully timed.

9. Propaganda must label events and people with distinctive phrases or slogans.

    a. They must evoke desired responses which the audience previously possesses

    b. They must be capable of being easily learned

    c. They must be utilized again and again, but only in appropriate situations

10. Propaganda must facilitate the displacement of aggression by specifying the targets for hatred.

11. Propaganda cannot immediately affect strong counter-tendencies; instead it must offer some form of action or diversion, or both.

12. Propaganda must evoke peoples' feelings over rationality, logic or reality.

Propaganda is alive and used well in every socialistic, dictatorial country in the world today (meaning in practically every country), and yes even in these United States where it is used to persuade people to support and elect stronger and stronger centralized power bases in Washington and state governments.

Understanding the use of propaganda provides the explanation as to why the definitions of freedom and liberty as used by left-leaning political factions are so diverse and counter-intuitive. Here is one simple example. On the one side it is argued that people should have the freedom to be able to obtain anything they want or need based on their own effort and ingenuity. And the other side argues that man should have the freedom from the want of hunger, from the lack of health care, or from the lack of adequate shelter. The latter argument rests upon the false notion that a centralized government should therefore be empowered to provide these needs, and it also relies upon an emotional, natural "feeling" (or notion of caring) of people by propagandizing the notions of fairness and equality. One side says 'freedom of..' the other says 'freedom from…', while both argue for 'freedom'.

The two sides are diametrically opposed to each other by definition and in reality while using the same word to describe their objective. Here is an actual case in point. Barack Obama, in a public debate on national television during the 2008 presidential campaign, was asked the following question: "Is health care of the people a privilege or a right?" His answer…."I believe health care is a right of the people, no question." (I paraphrased it). No one can argue against that, correct? All people should have the right to proper health care. But then he leaped across a chasm of logic (a chasm the size of the Grand Canyon) to assume by implication that government alone is authorized and obligated to provide that right to all the people. That the government should have that right was not explained or defended in his argument; it was moot and assumed, and the audience fell into line. But that was his meaning, as any socialist would understand.

And what was John McCain's response? He agreed, but argued for somewhat less of government involvement. And here is why John McCain was not the best or even a good candidate for the opposite party.

What McCain should have said, and what Ronald Reagan almost certainly would have said, is this: "Yes, I agree that all men have the right to health care and it should be their free right to obtain it in any manner and to what extent and in what quantity and at what price and at precisely the point in which they most need it; to be determined solely by themselves as they have a right to do. I do not believe that their rights should be handed over to a strong, central government to act as dictator over who will get health care and at what level and at what point and at whose cost they will get what health care they are adjudged to be entitled to. That, sir, is not freedom, that is societal slavery."

John McCain had a golden opportunity to expose the senseless propaganda being spouted by his opponent, and to teach the American people as to what freedom meant or should mean in this country. He either did not understand, or more likely, his hands were tied because he himself and most of his party as well, adhere to the notion that most all things can and should be provided by a strong central government. And since they are an advocate, only to a lesser degree than their opponents, they are not able to stand up for the rights of man...the rights of Liberty.

Liberty

CHAPTER 3

————•————

ENTITLEMENTS ARE DESTROYING FREEDOM

The Role of Government

As envisioned by the Founding Fathers, the primary role of the Federal Government was to provide protection of this country's people from aggression both from within as well as from without. There is more in the Constitution's structure designed to limit the powers of the government, than in allowing for its expansion. Knowing that world history was replete with governmental powers centered at the top governing from the top down, the Founders dedicated this new type of government founded upon the notion that only the people had the ultimate powers, and they were to be ruled or governed from the bottom up. Government should not be allowed to encroach upon the liberty of the people, not take on the role of dictator or be provider for the people's needs.

Over the past 100 years, beginning with Theodore Roosevelt and more importantly, Woodrow Wilson, the role of the American Government has been considerably changed and expanded. More and more, it has taken on the role of dictator with its many bureaucrats, agencies, regulations, and especially with the many entitlements doled out to the people.

Gradually, the American people have been conditioned to look to government for almost everything, including prosperity, economic stability and growth, job creation, deliverance from the lack of food, transportation, clothing, health care, from competition, from just about everything. Governmental mandate seems to be that there should be nothing that the federal government should not be doing for its people; it's just taking time until everyone falls into line. I know that sounds cynical, but listen to the rhetoric coming from Washington; the great preponderance of it centers on what government can or should be doing, rather than fighting for the freedoms of its people. This nation's government was founded on the notion that the central role of the federal government is to protect the freedoms of the people, first and foremost. In the last 100 years that role has been completely reversed. Creation of a utopian world which the left envisions, ensures the complete loss of the freedoms of its people, but that is where this country is headed and is the prevailing direction.

When President John F. Kennedy said in an inaugural address, "Ask not what your country can do for you; ask what you can do for your country", he struck a visceral sounding bell. It sounded good. In fact, it sounded great and has been quoted many times since. Unfortunately, it can be read in two different ways and has been seen in two diabolical opposites. Conservatives like the first part, since they favor less government. The left likes the second part in that it serves to support efforts to raise more taxes and for the people to sacrifice more for the benefit of the "country", i.e. the poor and downtrodden. The statement is classical propaganda and Kennedy, a liberal, used it with great effect.

Entitlement Programs
To legitimize the gravitation of power to the central government, politicians have relied heavily on the enactment and growth of entitlement programs; social security, Medicare, welfare, and bailouts to name a few. That fact today cannot be disputed. It is not the purpose of this book to enumerate in detail all these programs and describe their lack of legitimacy, birth, growth, corruption, current status, or their destiny to fail or succeed. Many people rely on them for survival. That they have grown to the point that most of the people have determined that they cannot live without them and that people

must automatically look to government to enlarge them, enact more of them, testifies that their existence has become "the opium of the people".

Government interventions never fail to fail. But the pervasive belief in their efficacy is no mystery. It's simply human nature. The French economist Frederic Bastiat said government is the great fiction by which everyone attempts to live at the expense of everyone else.

This nation was founded on great principles, one of the most important of which is that people have the right (the freedom) to succeed or fail, prosper or not, by what they through their own initiative and effort can achieve. Self-reliance is the call word. It means people can become wealthy or not as they themselves see fit. That notion, that freedom has been largely overshadowed, even destroyed in the clamor over redistribution and the growth of big government.

Entitlements Buy Votes…and Enslave people

That the promise of entitlements is being used to purchase the majority vote is beyond dispute. That its discovery is a latter-day phenomenon is a myth of astronomical proportion. The Founding Fathers were not naïve in their dreams and expectations of universal freedoms. They clearly understood the nature of men and their designs on governing people. Here are a few quotes that testify of that knowledge:

"They that can give up essential liberty to obtain a little temporary safety deserve neither liberty nor safety." -- *Benjamin Franklin*

"The greatest tyrannies are always perpetrated in the name of the noblest causes." -- Thomas Paine

Liberty

The issue today is the same as it has been throughout all history, whether man shall be allowed to govern himself or be ruled by a small elite." -- Thomas Jefferson

"The two enemies of the people are criminals and government, so let us tie the second down with the chains of the Constitution so the second will not become the legalized version of the first."-- Thomas Jefferson

"I have a right to nothing which another has a right to take away." -- Thomas Jefferson

"I believe there are more instances of the abridgement of freedoms of the people by gradual and silent encroachment of those in power than by violent and sudden usurpations." -- James Madison

When the people find that they can vote themselves money, that will herald the end of the republic. Benjamin Franklin

It is often said by the left, that the Constitution was born in an agrarian society, that those in that day did not, could not understand society as it exists today; and that the Constitution is a "living Document" meaning that it must change with the times, 'modern' times. Do the above quotes lead one to believe that nonsense? Don't these quotes demonstrate that the Founders in fact knew of what they had wrought in their day? And these quotes are merely a drop in the ocean of their understanding!

History Repeats Itself...The Governmental Cycle
There is nothing new under the sun. Great nations rise and fall. The people go from bondage to spiritual truth, to great courage, from courage to liberty, from liberty to abundance, from abundance to selfishness, from selfishness to complacency, from complacency to apathy,

from apathy to dependence, from dependence back again to bondage. Look at the history of just this nation alone and see if you don't see the direction, or vector at work in the following steps:

From Bondage to Spiritual Faith;
From Spiritual Faith to Courage;
From Courage to Freedom;
From Freedom to Abundance;
From Abundance to Selfishness;
From Selfishness to Complacency;
From Complacency to Apathy;
From Apathy to Fear;
From Fear to Dependency;
From Dependency to Bondage

The release of initiative and enterprise made possible by self-government ultimately generates disintegrating forces from within. Again and again, after freedom brings opportunity and some degree of plenty, the competent become selfish, luxury-loving and complacent; the incompetent and unfortunate grow envious and covetous; and all three groups turn aside from the hard road of freedom to worship the golden calf of economic security. The historical cycle seems to be well along in its course here in America.

America's Path to "Economic Security" is Unsustainable
Entitlement programs have bankrupted this nation as well as those so-called democratic countries in Europe and the rest of the world. The world is currently on the edge of a precipice of catastrophic proportions. Entitlements or the promise of them can simply no longer be supported by existing nor even vastly greater levels of additional taxations beyond the not-too-distant future. Without major, and I do mean major, reductions in entitlement programs (social security, Medicare and Medicaid, welfare, bailouts) these programs are destined to collapse from

their own weight. More on this is covered in Section 3, PROPERTY, but a few words related to Liberty merit consideration.

That America's national debt load and its corresponding proclivity to deficit spending, has placed this nation at the edge of bankruptcy is beginning to be well known among its people. There isn't a politician in Washington that doesn't know we are in major financial trouble and that something must be done about the major causes, i.e. entitlement programs. But guess what? There is also not a politician in or near Washington who is either willing or able to do anything about it!

Why is that so? Make room for a few facts.

1. A shrinking minority is carrying the tax burden. Right now 25% of all eligible voters pay almost 90% of the tax burden. Over 50% of eligible voters pay absolutely no income taxes.

2. A huge majority of voters in America have been conditioned or convinced that we must look to the government for all solutions to America's economic problems, (thanks to effective propaganda).

3. The vast majority of Americans in one way or another is either now, or will be, inextricably dependent on these entitlement programs, (via an aging population).

4. Class envy between the have-nots and those who have is being fostered and enflamed by the left, pitting the less fortunate against bankers, Wall Street, big business, and the 'wealthy', (thanks again to the propagandists).

So let me say it again. There is not a "sensible" politician in America who is willing to run on a campaign seriously advocating the reductions of entitlements. Oh they will give lip service to the need, or they will advocate raising taxes on those "most able" to pay but it is simply political suicide to argue otherwise...the actual reduction of that which is killing

America. The voters who pay little or no taxes (by now the vast majority) and who stand to benefit the most from the public largesse are not going to vote for the reduction or elimination of that to which they are dependent. Who can argue otherwise? Is this not the truth?

America has already arrived at the point in which Benjamin Franklin, Thomas Jefferson, John and Samuel Adams were warning about, where Liberty will be done away with. Just like what is now happening in Europe, there will be much civil unrest, yes even rioting in the streets of America when entitlements will have collapsed or be paid by dollars no longer worth anything.

However, this is not a book on economics where there could be much more said about the coming total devaluation of the world's fiat currencies. It is a book about the unalienable rights of man.

The Twisted Argument about Freedom and Equality

All men were created equal by God. That statement has a different meaning to different people. To the Founders and to most Americans who fought for this nation's freedom, it meant simply that all men were blessed with the right to live, the right to enjoy liberty and freedom, the right to pursue prosperity and happiness as defined by the dictates of one's own conscience and ambitions.

The left has redefined that concept of freedom so as to actually destroy the meaning of freedom as originally understood. Equality of man's God-given rights has been grossly, and grotesquely twisted to mean Equality of Outcomes. The difference plays on these two phrases: Freedom of.... And Freedom from....

Freedom <u>from</u> poverty, hunger, the lack of health care and all social injustices, are not translated into Liberty when the equality of outcome is demanded by force or threat of force. This is not Liberty or freedom at all. It is in fact tyranny. It is the road to serfdom as Friedrich Hayek said. Putting it more correctly, the left believes in equality, some having more equality than others. In a guaranteed system where redistribution, or leveling, i.e. the equality of outcomes is the objective, SUCH A SYSTEM ALWAYS REQUIRES THAT SOMEONE BE PUT INTO THE POSITION OF DETERMINING AND ENFORCING THE OUTCOMES. Both the haves and have-nots become enslaved. The former because they are forced to provide for the others, and the latter because they have become addicted to the entitlement. It is an insidious, pathetic position in that it is founded on emotional notions of "fairness" and is bolstered and "justified" with the art and lies of propaganda. "Anyone against social security wants people to die or survive eating dog food," the left is fond of saying and arguments like it.

The left believes, or at least argues, for equal outcomes, socialism, communism and the central control of society. That is not Freedom. That is what Liberty is not.

Edward Gibbon, the great Roman and Greek historian offered this analysis of both their downfalls:

"In the end, more than they wanted freedom, they wanted security. They wanted a comfortable life, and they lost it all -- security, comfort, and freedom. When ... the freedom they wished for was freedom from responsibility, then Athens ceased to be free."

CHAPTER 4

━━━●━━━

WHAT FREEDOM IS

Freedom in America is all-inclusive, meaning that it includes more than Life, Liberty and the Pursuit of Happiness. Additional unalienable rights not listed in the Declaration of Independence are:

The right of self government.
The right to bear arms for self-defense.
The right to own, develop, enjoy the fruits of, and dispose of property.
The right to make personal choices.
The right of free conscience.
The right to choose a mate.
The right to beget one's kind.
The right to assemble.
The right to petition.
The right to free speech.
The right to a free press.
The right to enjoy the fruits of one's labors.
The right to improve one's position through barter, purchase, and sale.
The right to contrive and invent.
The right to explore and use the natural resources of the earth.
The right to privacy.
The right to provide personal security.
The right to a fair trial.
The right of free association.
The right to contract.
The right to a choice of religion.

Liberty

Someone once said that freedom is the right to fail. By that it also means the right to succeed. But what freedom means to a nation of people is more than this. Thomas Jefferson said it well,

"The issue today is the same as it has been throughout all history, whether man shall be allowed to govern himself or be ruled by a small elite."

Another quote from Jefferson:

"To take from one because it is thought that his own industry and that of his father's has acquired too much, in order to spare to others, who, or whose fathers have not exercised equal industry and skill, is to violate arbitrarily the first principle of association--the guarantee to every one of a free exercise of his industry and the fruits acquired by it."

Another quote relevant to the point:

"A people may prefer a free government, but if, from indolence, or carelessness, or cowardice, or want of public spirit, they are unequal to the exertions necessary for preserving it; if they will not fight for it when it is directly attacked; if they can be deluded by the artifices used to cheat them out of it; if by momentary discouragement, or temporary panic, or a fit of enthusiasm for an individual, they can be induced to lay their liberties at the feet even of a great man, or trust him with powers which enable him to subvert their institutions; in all these cases they are more or less unfit for liberty: and though it may be for their good to have had it even for a short time, they are unlikely long to enjoy it." -- John Stuart Mill, Representative Government, 1861

Every man is guaranteed by the Constitution equal protection under the law. Freedom is a right granted to man (but not by men) and in America it is to be guaranteed and protected by its Constitution.

Free agency means the exercise of the will, the power to choose. Freedom means the power and privilege to carry out our choices.

The War in Heaven

In man's pre-mortal existence, amongst all of God's children, there arose a war of great proportion. A war of words ensued, involving among other things the free agency of man. On the one hand, it was argued that man, in coming to earth to be tested, should be allowed his complete freedom to choose right or wrong in his mortal existence. That freedom of choice could result in success and, of course, failure.

The leader of the opposition argued that it would not be fair if some were to fail and thereby not be able to achieve the ultimate benefits and rewards of the mortal experience, i.e. be able to return to the Father's presence. That leader argued for equality of outcome. Therefore the leader of this argument claimed that he would assure "that not one would be lost". But along with that assurance, the free agency of man would be abrogated, lost, destroyed. And God said that "(he) *rebelled against me, and sought to destroy the agency of man, which I, the Lord God, had given him, and also, that I should give unto him mine own power; ..."* And he became known as the father of all lies from that time forth, to lead men captive who will not hearken to the voice of God. And he and his followers were cast out.

I do believe that that war continues to rage on earth, especially today and especially in America. The left hammers home the "fairness" doctrine which continues to be preached and fostered by a plethora of lies, half-truths, and great sounding propaganda. We need to choose sides and to be a force for good and correct principles.

So What are We to Do?
We need to constantly battle for Freedom.

In light of all we see happening in this country and the world today, many are wont to ask, "What are we to do, and what can be done to protect and restore our Freedoms being taken away"? The answer is threefold:

1. Vote. Make your feelings and beliefs known in the ballet box. People who don't vote cannot be legitimate complainers, nor can they expect to have any influence in causing change.

2. Fight the battle with words and ideas. Stand up for liberty and freedom; at home, in public, in school, in every walk of life where you tread. Teach, counsel, and explain the truth. And dispute error wherever and whenever you encounter it.

3. Be prepared to defend Freedom with force of arms when necessary. The time when that may be necessary within the borders of this Country is probably very likely to occur in our lifetimes. Not that we would need to do battle against foreign aggression, but against enemies within our borders and of our own numbers.

CHAPTER 5

⸻ ◉ ⸻

AMERICA'S FORM OF GOVERNMENT

...of the People, by the People, and for the People.

"Democracy is two wolves and a lamb voting on what to have for lunch. Liberty is a well-armed lamb contesting the vote."
Benjamin Franklin

The Miracle at Philadelphia

The Constitutional Convention held in Philadelphia between May 14 and September 17, 1787, was conducted in secret behind closed doors. People were most anxious to know what form of government would emerge from these proceedings. The final vote was neither unanimous nor were all the delegates of similar mind. There was much contention and disagreement.

The most contentious disputes revolved around the apportionment of the senate (by state or population), method of election for senators, how "proportional representation" was to be defined (whether to include slaves or other property), whether to divide the executive power between three persons or

59

divest the power into a single president, how to elect the president, how long his term was to be and whether he could stand for reelection, what offenses should be impeachable, the nature of a fugitive slave clause, whether to allow the abolition of the slave trade, and whether judges should be chosen by the legislature or executive. Most of the time during the convention was spent on deciding these issues, while the powers of legislature, executive, and judiciary were not heavily disputed. Once the convention began, the delegates first agreed on the principles of the convention, and then they agreed on Madison's Virginia plan and began to modify it. A Committee of Detail assembled during the July 4 recess and produced a rough draft. Most of this rough draft remained in place, and can be found in the final version of the constitution. After the final issues were resolved, the Committee on Style produced the final version, and it was voted on and sent to the states. There were 55 delegates, 39 of which signed.

Much of the disagreement stemmed from the lack of a Bill of Rights, which was later agreed to and added to the Constitution.

The miracle was multi-faceted. More than anything, however, was that never before had a government been forged in this manner that would be used to govern a free people as large as America was, even then. What kind of a government was it? Benjamin Franklin was first to describe it. When he emerged from the proceedings on the final day and walked back into the public view a woman standing nearby asked him, "Well Mr. Franklin, what kind of a government have you decided for us?" To which he replied, "A Republic ma'am, if you can keep it!"

America is NOT a Democracy
Guess what? America is not a Democracy and should not be referred to as such. America is a Democratic Republic. It

operates on democratic principles, but it is not a Democracy. It is a Republic.

All Forms of Government

On this scale all forms of government can be positioned.

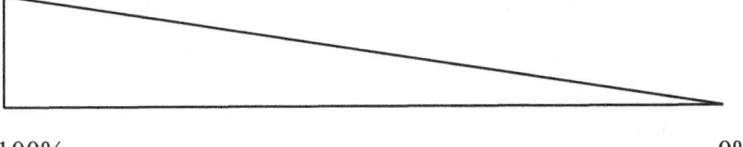

100%   0%

As we have seen throughout history almost every government of man has been firmly entrenched towards the left end. Perhaps that is why the term "left" is used to describe those who favor more government.

Somewhere in the left quadrant is found these forms of government:

Socialism
Communism
Nazism
Fascism
Dictatorships
Kings
Emperors

Democracy is generally defined as a form of government in which all adult citizens have an equal say in the decisions that affect their lives. Ideally, this includes equal (and more or less direct) participation in the proposal, development and passage of legislation into law. By definition, the majority rules in all matters. Majority rule is the main characteristic of a democracy. It is, therefore, possible and also probable for a minority to be oppressed by a "tyranny of the majority" in the absence of governmental or constitutional protections of individual or group rights.

A republic is a form of government in which the people, or some significant portion of them, have supreme control over the government and where offices of state are (supposedly) elected or chosen by its people. I say supposedly because there have been and still are sovereign countries calling themselves republics, such as The Union of Soviet Socialist Republics, but which are anything but republics. A true republic is one of representative government where people are <u>freely</u> elected to high office by all the people and where the elected represent the interests of the people who elected them.

Both modern and ancient republics vary widely in their ideology and composition. In classical and medieval times the archetype of all republics was the Roman Republic, which existed in Rome between the period when it had kings, and the periods when it had emperors. In modern republics such as the United States, the executive is legitimized both by a constitution and by popular suffrage.

The American Form of Government
The American Revolution began as a rejection only of the authority of British parliament over the colonies, not of the monarchy. The failure of the British monarch to protect the colonies from what they considered the infringement of their rights to representative government, the monarch's branding of those requesting redress as traitors, and his support for sending combat troops to demonstrate authority resulted in widespread

recognition of the British monarchy as tyrannical. With the United States Declaration of Independence the leaders of the revolt firmly rejected the monarchy and embraced republicanism. The leaders of the revolution were well versed in the writings of the French liberal thinkers and also the history of the classical republics. John Adams had notably written a book on republics throughout history. In addition, the widely distributed and popularly read-aloud tract *Common Sense*, by Thomas Paine, succinctly and eloquently laid out the case for republican ideals and independence to the larger public. The Constitution of the United States ratified in 1789 created a relatively strong federal republic. The first ten amendments to the Constitution, called the United States Bill of Rights, guaranteed certain natural rights fundamental to republican ideals that justified the Revolution. The American Republic is grounded on a true, protected popular vote system.

The American system is defined by its separation of powers balanced between the three pillars of governance; The Executive, The Legislative, and the Judicial branches of government. They are structured and designed, first and foremost, to protect the rights of every citizen, and to be limited in scope and power. That is America's Form of Government.

Liberty

———●———

CHAPTER 6

FREEDOM REQUIRES A MORAL PEOPLE

"Only a virtuous people are capable of freedom. As nations become more corrupt and vicious, they have more need of masters." Benjamin Franklin

Freedom cannot survive and thrive with a dishonest populace. When greed, avarice, dishonesty and corruption spread like an uncontrollable cancer, a society cannot freely function and will eventually collapse into civil chaos, civil disobedience, war and then taken over by dictatorships ruling by tyrannical force. "Force always attracts men of low morality," said Albert Einstein.

Somerset Maugham said, "If a nation values anything more than freedom, it will lose its freedom; and the irony of it is that if it is comfort or money that it values more, it will lose that too."

Somewhere in the cycle from enslavement to freedom and back again, moral corruption envelopes society and begins the downward spiral towards its downfall. The only thing that can perpetuate freedom is a powerful certitude from within people to be obedient to even rudimentary moral principles. That is how and why freedom can exist among men. It is simply impossible for freedom to survive when people cannot live moral lives.

The Ten Commandments

The Ten Commandments represent these most basic, rudimentary laws upon which a free society can exist. It is not coincidental that they are some of God's laws, because man's freedom is a conditional gift from him. Conditional based upon obedience to God's laws. Obedience to God's laws and freedom are inseparable. These Ten Commandments most certainly are not all the laws God has given to which men should be obedient. But they should be cherished by a freedom-loving people as being necessary to guide society and to ensure their freedom. And obedience to them should be recognized by all men as absolutely, inextricably connected to their freedom.

They are found in Exodus Chapter 20. And here they are:

1. *Thou shalt have no other Gods before me.*
2. *Thou shalt not make unto thee any graven image (idol worship).*
3. *Thou shalt not take the name of the Lord thy God in vain.*
4. *Remember the Sabbath day, to keep it holy.*
5. *Honor thy father and thy mother.*
6. *Thou shalt not kill.*
7. *Thou shalt not commit adultery.*
8. *Thou shalt not steal.*
9. *Thou shalt not bear false witness.*
10. *Thou shalt not covet… anything that is thy neighbor's.*

These commandments should be in every legislative house, every courtroom, every school, and in every home in America. They do not represent a church or special religion, per se. They represent a true, moral, social order. All men should observe them, be obedient to them, and teach them to their children as their contribution towards a free society.

God has promised that if men keep His commandments, their freedoms will be protected. He has also promised if they do not, they will lose their freedoms and be reduced to captivity and enslavement. It has always been so and it will always be.

The Cycle of Liberty and The Cycle of Spiritual Morality
The cycle of liberty has already been described in a previous chapter as it pertains to socio-economic ebbs and flows. There is also a similar cycling involving the spiritual morality of man down through time, the details of which are well documented and recorded in the vast collections of scriptures made available to us today. That cycle is briefly outlined and matched up with the socio-economic cycle as follows:

The Cycle of Liberty	Spiritual Morality Cycle
From Bondage to Spiritual Faith;	Spiritual darkness, bondage
From Spiritual Faith to Courage;	Humility, realization of sin
From Courage to Freedom;	Repentance leads to belief
From Freedom to Abundance;	Righteousness prevails
From Abundance to Selfishness;	Selfishness/Greed enter in
From Selfishness to Complacency;	Man ignores word of God
From Complacency to Apathy;	Apostasy enters and grows
From Apathy to Fear;	Unrighteousness abounds
From Fear to Dependency;	Spiritual darkness prevails
From Dependency to Bondage	Men are in bondage again

These two cycles are inextricably connected and confirm the notion that you cannot have freedom when the people are dishonest and immoral. When the high moral code is abridged and distrust, dishonesty, cheating on spouses and families, the lack of social respect, corruption and more abounds, freedom cannot and will not prevail. It will be destroyed, taken away, lost.

God has said over and over again through his prophets, speaking to mankind in general, *"If ye keep my commandments, ye shall prosper in the land."* It will always be so.

America is losing its Freedoms

America is losing its freedoms…and its spiritual and moral integrity as well. Socialism and the left, in showing that they "care" and in trying to legislate charity to the "poor, down-trodden, and the less fortunate" and through the courts, by legal means, force people to be "charitable" have been instrumental in destroying America's freedoms. In the past the watch word has been "creeping socialism". Today it is more like galloping socialism. When a vast portion of the Gross Domestic Product (GDP), involving health care, is now controlled by the federal government and through entitlement and countless other programs that are choking this country's prosperity are in fact enslaving America, the people without realizing it are losing their freedoms in a very big way. And at the same time their moral turpitude is forging the direction towards moral decay.

Consider these alarming facts in America today:

1. A vast majority of Americans believe or tolerate "at will" abortions as merely a means of birth-control destroying the notion of the sanctity of life.
2. Dishonesty, cheating on taxes and spouses, corruption in familial relationships, the majority of all children now being born out of wedlock; these and more are all being treated as acceptable social behavior.
3. People are less willing to undertake personal responsibility and look to others, or the government to provide.
4. Crime levels and prisons are at a very high level and growing.

5. There is more and more crime at high levels in both government and business.
6. There is a preponderance of "Politically Correct Speaking" control which is choking off people's right to free speech.
7. Major crime is being allowed and forgiven through means of legislative amnesty and from ignorance.
8. Schools are forbidden by law of even mentioning the belief in God or faith in Him in the nation's classrooms.
9. Our children are taught in classrooms every day that truth is relative and not absolute.

The list is long, and growing.

Where is America on the two cycles? Go back and look at the two lists and see what you come up with. You be the judge.

America's Culture in the beginning

Dennis Prager, popular conservative talk-show host, commentator, and social philosopher, in describing the culture of America, speaks of the "American Trinity", which he believes consists of these three pillars noted on every U. S. coin:

1. Liberty
2. In God we trust
3. E Pluribus Unum (out of many, one).

We are not African-American, Italian-American, Mexican-American, Asian American, Scottish-American, not any Ethno-American…we are all Americans. Our strength is not through diversity, it is through unity. And on these three pillars rests the culture of America.

Liberty

Mr. Prager was once asked while giving an audience, "In your opinion, what is the greatest problem facing America right now?" His response;

"The greatest tragedy in America today is that we are not passing along to our children what it means to be an American."

Will this always be America's culture? With the grace of God and through the will and righteousness of the American people, it will. At least that is our hope.

SECTION THREE
PROPERTY

"Life and Liberty are secure only so long as the Rights of Property are secure."   Thomas Jefferson

"I have a right to nothing which another has a right to take away."   Thomas Jefferson

"Private property is the most important guarantee of freedom."   F. A. Hayek

"Property must be secured, or liberty cannot exist."   John Adams

The rights to Life, Liberty and Property do not exist because men have made laws. On the contrary, it was the fact that life, liberty, and property rights existed beforehand that caused men in America to make laws for the protection of these rights in the first place.

Property rights are sacred because they are also a gift of God the same as all other unalienable rights of man are gifts of God.

"The sacred rights of property are to be guarded at every point. I call them sacred, because, if they are unprotected, all other rights become worthless or visionary. What is personal liberty,

if it does not draw after it the right to enjoy the fruits of our own industry? What is political liberty, if it imparts only perpetual poverty to us and all our posterity? What is the privilege of a vote, if the majority of the hour may sweep away the earnings of our whole lives, to gratify the rapacity of the indolent, the cunning, or the profligate, who are borne into power upon the tide of a temporary popularity?"

Judge Joseph Story, 1851

What is Property

The word "property" itself has several unique and differentiated meanings. In general, however, it refers to a thing or things owned; tools, natural resources, real estate, money, writings, patents, business entities, holdings, possessions, everything. Property entails ownership then, and the rights to ownership of things. Property is used in the satisfaction of needs; first with overcoming hunger, then providing clothing and shelter, and proceeding into the building of dams, bridges, highways, transportation, electricity and so forth. Indeed property and property rights are connected to just about everything we use or do.

Capitalism is the unfettered natural order of human survival

As with the man who needed a better way of catching fish than with his bare hands, who designed and built pole, hook, line, and sinker by using his free industry and property that he owned or bargained for, capitalism became the natural order of things.

Capitalism is the economic system in which all or most of the means of production and distribution (such as land, factories, railroads, etc.) are privately owned and operated for profit under fully competitive conditions. That is the meaning of capitalism. When any other social order is forced on man designed to level the outcome of man's productivity, man's freedom is abrogated.

Without the imposition of any organized social order which removes man's right of property by force and thus deprives him of his freedom, man is free to achieve the highest level of prosperity as he naturally can and only the sky is the limit.

Property

Chapter 1

---⊖---

The Historical Battle
for Property Rights

Name any battle waged between men in the entire history of the world and at its root will be a fight over property. Whoever holds the power of property rights by force, holds control over other men. And gaining the power of property rights by force has been throughout history almost the entire story of man's existence.

Oh for sure, there have been arms length transactions between kings, magistrates, nobles, landed elites or governments of all kinds, but only very rarely, have property rights been freely controlled by individuals, even though that is the natural order of things.

Property rights in simple terms include the following three elements:

1. The right of ownership
2. The free right of use and to the fruits thereof
3. The right of transfer

Real Property Rights
PROPERTY RIGHTS: *The right to life is the source of all rights—and the right to property is their only implementation. Without property rights, no other rights are possible. Since man has to sustain his life by his own effort, the man who has no right to the product of his effort has no means to sustain his life. The man who produces while others dispose of his product is a slave.*   Ayn Rand

Property

Real property (or real estate) refers to land and the resources which exist upon or in the land. It is by far the most important of all property rights. Throughout history the rights of certain individual personal property such as swords, teepees, or say a cow have pretty much been respected and honored universally by most societies. It is upon real property where most battles have been waged and where individual rights have been trampled upon.

When speaking of the battle for property there should be this important distinction: On the one hand, battles between armies of kings, nobles, etc. and on the other, the singular, universal battle for individual, sovereign rights. It is the latter, being far more important and real, that deserves the most attention.

Putting it very simply we are speaking about whether man has total freedom or is a slave to others. On a continuum at the left is absolutely no personal control of property, or slavery, and on the other end is 100% control or freedom.

Slavery   Freedom
0%   100%

Throughout most of history the status of property rights has been distinctly tilted towards the left. Property rights have been forcefully controlled by the powerful and by powerful I don't mean economically, per se. I mean kings, nobles, magistrates, emperors and popes, by the force of arms. The common man has had little or no rights of property.

Social Classes helps distinguish
Property Rights
Kings and emperors held ultimate ownership, others such as nobles, magistrates, etc. held lesser ownerships, and common individuals held little or no ownership. To distinguish where people fell on that scale it was common to fit people into

classes; classes which were nearly impossible to graduate from unless, of course, one could amass a greater armed force to acquire more property rights which almost never occurred.

For the most part, there have been three major classes or estates: 1. Those who rule (The Aristocracy; Kings, Emperors, the Church), 2. Those who fight and administrate (The Middle Classes; the nobility), and 3. Those who work (The skilled and unskilled workers; peasants, commoners, and the poor).

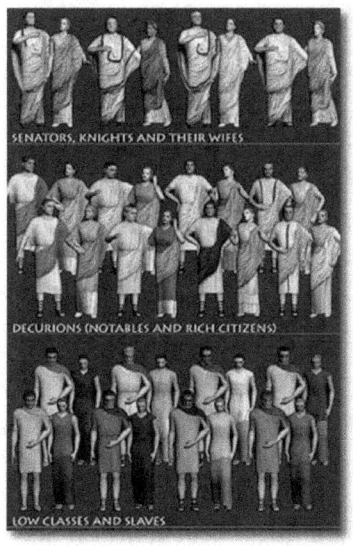

Within that class structure property rights were carefully and forcefully controlled at the top and the middle with little or no property rights extending to the masses in the lower classes. And to build the castles, the cathedrals, the roads and canals, and the pyramids, the upper classes used the lower classes by heavy conscription or forced labor to build their empires. The lower classes have languished throughout time having little to call their own except their clothing, weapons, and meager hovels to live in and raise their children. Real property rights to most people have been non-existent.

This basic hierarchical structure, comprising the "upper classes," the "middle classes," the "Working Classes" (with skilled laborers at one extreme and unskilled at the other), and the impoverished "Under Class," remained relatively stable despite periodic (and frequently violent) upheavals. A modified class structure clearly remains in existence today in many parts of the world. However property rights are clearly not the same, quite fortunately, because of reasons related to the Renaissance, the Industrial Revolution and more importantly the birth of the U. S. Constitution.

Feudalism: Property rights of the Few
Although not always called that throughout history, Feudalism or Manorialism has been the system employed to restrict property rights to the middle and upper classes.

Serfdom is the status of peasants under feudalism. It was a condition of bondage or modified slavery which developed primarily during the High Middle Ages in Europe and lasted to the mid-19th century. Serfdom included the labor of serfs occupying a plot of land owned by a lord of the manor in return for protection and justice and the right to exploit certain fields within the manor to maintain their own subsistence. Serfdom involved not only work in the lord's fields, but his mines, forests and roads. The manor formed the basic unit of society and the Lord of the Manor and his serfs were bound legally, economically, and socially. Serfs were laborers who were bound to the land; they formed the lowest social class of the feudal society. Serfs were also defined as people in whose labor landowners held property rights.

To become a serf was a commitment that encompassed all aspects of the serf's life. Moreover, the condition of serfdom was inherited at birth. By taking on the duties of serfdom, serfs bound not only themselves but all of their future progeny.

The Right of Private Property Awakens
Increasing unrest and uprisings by serfs and peasants put pressure on the nobility and the clergy to reform the system. As a result serf and peasant demands were accommodated to some extent by the gradual establishment of new forms of land leases and increased personal liberties.

Property

An important factor in the decline of serfdom was industrial development — especially the Industrial Revolution. With the growing profitability of industry, farmers wanted to move to towns to receive higher wages than those they could earn working in the fields, while landowners also invested in the more profitable industry.

The era of the French Revolution (1790s to 1820s) saw serfdom abolished in most of Europe, except Russia and Austria. And in France, on August 11, 1789 with the "Decree Abolishing the Feudal System", the manorial system was abolished completely. It abolished the authority of manorial courts, outlawed pigeon houses, eliminated and altered tithes (set taxes), and freed those who were enslaved. The majority of the population consisted of peasants. This social system was no longer viable.

By the sixteenth century, it was clear that the crown's authority stopped where private property began. The ideas of individual sovereignty and individual proprietorship became entrenched in the common law of Britain and subsequently in the Constitution of the United States.

Just as hunting and gathering gave way to settled agriculture, settled agriculture gave way to the Industrial Revolution. That transition required secure property rights to capital assets in order to guarantee private investors a return on their investments. The rise of contractual arrangements such as the modern corporation and the growth of impersonal markets depended on protection of capital from governments by constitutions and from fellowmen by civil laws. The authors of the U.S. Declaration of Independence and the Constitution shared John Locke's and Adam Smith's beliefs in the importance of private ownership. The Founding Fathers firmly believed that the human right to private property had to be protected in law as the basis for individual liberty, a free society, and a free economy.

Let me enlarge upon that. The Founding Fathers firmly believed that the right of property was an unalienable right granted to man by his God. It is a sacred right, a right which allows man the freedom to accomplish whatever he sets his mind to, giving him the tools whereby accomplishment can be realized.

The Fifth Amendment to the Constitution was aimed at protecting private property from governmental takings. Because the rule of law and constitutions guaranteed the sanctity of property in England and the United States during the eighteenth and nineteenth centuries, trade and commerce flourished and economies grew, but again, I get ahead of myself.

CHAPTER 2

═══●═══

AMERICAN EXCEPTIONALISM

Property rights of common individuals faced the dawn of modern history ready to emerge as one of the greatest forces in all of history with the inception of the U. S. Constitution. In fact, it is at the root of what is known as American Exceptionalism.

American exceptionalism refers to the idea that the United States is qualitatively different from other countries. In this view, America's exceptionalism stems from its emergence from a revolution, becoming "the first new nation," and developing a uniquely American ideology, based on liberty, egalitarianism, individualism, populism and laissez-faire. This observation can be traced to the Frenchman Alexis de Tocqueville, the first writer to describe the United States as "exceptional" in 1831 and 1840. Historian Gordon Wood has argued, "Our beliefs in liberty, equality, constitutionalism, and the well-being of ordinary people came out of the Revolutionary era. So too did our idea that we Americans are a special people with a special destiny to lead the world toward liberty and democratic republicanism."

Of course, these ideals did not originate with us here in America, but in fact really had their beginnings in Britain and Northern Europe originating perhaps first in King Henry the 2nd's era with the development of British Common Law, and rights solidified later in the Magna Charta (1215).

The ideas that created the American Revolution were derived from a tradition of republicanism that had been repudiated by the British mainstream. Thomas Paine's *Common Sense* for the first time expressed the belief that America was not just an extension of Europe but a new land, a country of nearly unlimited potential and opportunity that had outgrown the British mother country. These sentiments laid the intellectual foundations for the Revolutionary concept of American exceptionalism and were closely tied to republicanism, the belief that sovereignty belonged to the people, and not to a hereditary ruling class.

Also, religious freedom characterized the American Revolution in unique ways—at a time when major nations had state religions. Republicanism (led by Thomas Jefferson and James Madison) created modern constitutional republicanism, with a limit on ecclesiastical powers practiced in Europe and elsewhere. Historian Thomas Kidd (2010) argues, "With the onset of the revolutionary crisis, a major conceptual shift convinced Americans across the theological spectrum that God was raising up America for some special purpose." Kidd further argues that "a new blend of Christian and republican ideology led religious traditionalists to embrace wholesale the concept of republican virtue." The birth of real, lasting freedom, hence, originated in the Americas.

Jefferson envisaged America becoming the world's great "empire of liberty"--that is, the model for democracy and republicanism. He identified his nation as a beacon to the world, for he said on departing the presidency in 1809, America was:

"Trusted with the destinies of this solitary republic of the world, the only monument of human rights, and the sole depository of the sacred fire of freedom and self-government, from hence it is to be lighted up in other regions of the earth, if other regions of the earth shall ever become susceptible of its benign influence."

Property

In a land full of rich, bounteous resources of all kinds, and a country guaranteeing full individual property rights, a land filling with people longing to be free, people who yearned to have the freedom to build anything their hearts desired; it is no wonder that prosperity exploded onto the world scene from this part of the world. Prosperity available to all but never before seen nor heard of in all of the world's history. God said this land "…is a land choice above all the earth."

Freedom and Self-Government is Sacred
Little did Jefferson know that the "…fire of freedom and self-government,,," was in very deed, sacred. The U. S. Constitution was inspired of God as God Himself explained in these words:

"According to the laws and constitution of the people, which I have suffered to be established, and should be maintained for the rights and protection of all flesh, according to just and holy principles; That every man may act in doctrine and principle pertaining to futurity, according to the moral agency which I have given unto him, that every man may be accountable for his own sins in the day of judgment.

"Therefore, it is not right that any man should be in bondage one to another.

"And for this purpose have I established the Constitution of this land, by the hands of wise men whom I raised up unto this very purpose, and redeemed the land by the shedding of blood." *(D&C 101:77-80)*

Human beings should not and must not become property to another human being to any degree or stretch of the meaning of the word against his will. That all men should be enjoined together for mutual protection from enemies and illegal encroachments and be required by force of law to participate in the cost of this protection is perfectly acceptable and desirable. All have a stake in that protection, but that is where the limits should be drawn. Men are dragged into bondage when they are required by force of law to provide the necessities of life to others regardless of the perceived sanctity of others needs or desires. In that action and by that encroachment, men come under bondage and that is against the U. S. Constitution, the rights of a free people, and the intent of the Great Creator.

The Free Market System Explodes
onto the World's Stage

American exceptionalism is perhaps no better illustrated than by the inception and explosion of popularity of the free market system first practiced on this continent beginning somewhat before 1776. By 1905 the United States had become the richest industrial nation in the world. With only 5 percent of the earth's continental land area and merely 6 percent of the world's population, the American people were producing over half of almost everything---clothes, food, houses, transportation, communications even luxuries. It is a great tribute to the brilliance of the Founding Fathers and to writers and thinkers such as John Locke and Adam Smith. But it is by far a greater tribute to what a free people with the full freedom of property rights can do when given those rights unfettered.

The Founding Fathers were fascinated with the possibility of setting up a political, social, and even economic structure based on natural law. As far as the economic element was concerned, they were profoundly influenced by a scholarly book written by Adam Smith, a college professor in Scotland, in 1776 called *The Wealth of Nations.*

Like a hand in a glove, this brilliant work fit into the thinking, experience, and nation-building philosophy the Founders were dreaming of developing. Thomas Jefferson wrote: "In political economy, I think Smith's *Wealth of Nations* the best book extant". (Bergh, Writings of Thomas Jefferson, 8:31.)

The United States was the first nation of people to undertake the structuring of a whole national economy on the basis of natural law and the free-market concept described by Adam Smith. Among other things, this formula calls for the following:

1. Specialized production---Let each person or corporation of persons do what they do best.
2. Exchange of goods and services takes place in a free-market environment without governmental or tyrannical interference in production, prices, or wages.
3. The free market provides most efficiently and completely the needs of the people on the basis of supply and demand, with no government-imposed monopolies.
4. Prices and control of resources are naturally regulated by free competition on the basis of supply and demand.
5. Profits are looked upon as the means by which production of goods and services is made worthwhile and rewarding, as well as the means to provide the capital necessary for research and development of still more goods and services needed by people. Expansion of business can only be accomplished through wise use of profits in the long run.
6. Competition provides the means by which quality is improved, quantity is increased, and prices are reduced.

The Proper Role of Government
in a Free Market

The Founding Fathers agreed with Adam Smith that the greatest threat to economic prosperity is the arbitrary intervention of government into the economic affairs of private business and the buying public. Historically this interference usually involved fixing of prices, fixing wages, controlling production, granting, protecting and even creating monopolies, or subsidizing special interests, products or market segments.

There are, however, some legitimate, needed and desirable areas of governmental responsibilities in the market place which belong to government. Some of them are:

1. PREVENTING ILLEGAL FORCE in the market place to compel purchase or sale of products or services.
2. PROTECTING THE PROPERTY RIGHTS of individuals and corporations from illegal confiscation by individuals, foreign entities, corporations or by government itself.
3. FERRETING OUT AND PREVENTING FRAUD in the misrepresentation of quality, location, or ownership of the item being sold or purchased.
4. BREAKING UP AND PREVENTING STRANGLING MONOPOLIES which eliminate competition and result in the restraint of trade. And above all the government should not itself create, promote or perpetuate or protect monopolies, period.
5. PREVENTING AND RESTRAINING DEBAUCHERY of the cultural standards and moral fiber of society by commercial exploitation of vice—pornography, obscenity, drugs, liquor, prostitution, or commercial gambling.

CHAPTER 3

—————————◉—————————

THE SECURING OF
PROPERTY RIGHTS

Life and Liberty are Secure Only so long as the Rights of Property are Secure

Property, per se, has no rights. Land, a hammer, a printing press, a horse, have no rights. They all exist for the benefit of man as he sees fit. Property rights, therefore, belong to man. John Locke, in his Second Essay Concerning Civil Government said,

"God, who hath given the world to men in common, hath also given them reason to make use of it to the best advantage of life and convenience."

If there were no such thing as "ownership" of property, meaning legally protected and exclusiveness, there would be no reason to make use of it to the best advantage of life and convenience. Without private "rights" in developed, improved, or created property, it would be perfectly lawful for a lazy, covetous neighbor to move in as soon as the improvements were completed and take possession of the fruits of his industrious neighbor. And even then, the covetous neighbor would not be secure, because someone stronger than he could thereafter take it away from him.

Property rights, therefore, must be secure for without them it would completely destroy the incentive of an industrious person to develop, improve, or create any more property.

A Person's Property is a Projection of Life Itself

All property is an extension of a person's life, energy, and ingenuity. Therefore, to confiscate or destroy such property of another is, in reality, an attack on the essence of life itself. The person who has worked to cultivate his land, obtained his house by hard labor, created a beautiful watch, or secured a wage by his labor, has projected his very being—the very essence of his life—into that labor. A threat to his property, therefore, is a threat to the very essence of his life.

That is exactly how John Locke saw it when he said:

"Though the earth and all inferior creatures be common [as gifts from God] to all men, yet every man has a "property" in his own "person". This, nobody has any right to but himself. The "labour" of his body and the "work" of his hands, we may say, are properly his. Whatsoever, then, he removes out of the state that Nature hath provided and left it in, he hath mixed his labour with it, and joined to it something that is his own, and thereby makes it his property...

"He that is nourished by the acorns he picked up under an oak, or the apples he gathered from the trees in the wood, has certainly appropriated them to himself. Nobody can deny but the nourishment is his. I ask, then, when did they begin to be his? When he digested? Or when he ate? Or when he boiled? Or when he brought them home? Or when he picked them up? And it is plain, if the first gathering made them not his, nothing else could. "

Property Rights and the Right to Life and Liberty are Bound Together

Justice George Sutherland of the U. S. Supreme Court once told the New York State Bar Association:

"It is not the right of property which is protected, but the right to property. Property, per se, has no rights; but the individual—the man—has three great rights, equally sacred from arbitrary interference: the right to his LIFE, the right to his LIBERTY, the right to his PROPERTY... The three rights are so bound together as to be essentially one right. To give a man his life but deny him his liberty, is to take from him all that makes his life worth living. To give him his liberty but take from him the property which is the fruit and badge of his liberty, is to still leave him a slave." (Principle or Expedient? Annual Address to the New York State Bar Association, 21 January 1921, p. 18.)

What we are really talking about here is that man has every right to the fruits of his labors. It cannot, rather should not be forcefully taken from him without his consent. To do so is to bring him under bondage. What that means therefore, is that every man has the right to be rich or not. Abraham Lincoln had this to say about that:

"Property is the fruit of labor. Property is desirable, is a positive good in the world. That some should be rich shows that others may become rich and hence is just encouragement to industry and enterprise. Let not him who is houseless pull down the house of another, but let him work diligently to build one for himself, thus by example assuring that his own shall be safe from violence....I take it that it is best for all to leave each man free to acquire property as fast as he can. Some will get wealthy. I don't believe in a law to prevent a man from getting rich; it would do more harm than good." (Quoted in The Freeman: Ideas on Liberty, May 1955, p.7)

And finally, John Adams made it clear that property rights are essential to Liberty and Freedom. He said:

"The moment the idea is admitted into society that property is not as sacred as the laws of God, and that there is not a force of

Property

law and public justice to protect it, anarchy and tyranny commence. Property must be secured or Liberty cannot exist." (Charles Francis Adams, ed., The Works of John Adams, 10 vols. 6:9, 280)

CHAPTER 4

———●———

EQUALITY

If welfare and equality are to be primary aims of law, some people must necessarily possess a greater power of coercion in order to force redistribution of material goods. Political power alone should be equal among human beings: yet striving for other kinds of equality absolutely requires political inequality."

Tibor Machan

E Pluribus Unum is the motto of the United States. That is to say, out of many.....one. In other words, this nation is a nation without class distinction. It is a nation filled with people from all around the world, from all nations, from all walks of life, and from all ranks, colors, ethnicities, and religions. All have been welcomed in controlled numbers and encouraged to join and blend in. No one, by reason of the law, should be restricted because of any of these distinctions. Any person is just as much "an American" as any other. The intent is to eliminate from the social order, the nobles, the elites, the commoners; the formal recognition of some elevated by rank over others either by birth, by race, by religion, by gender, by wealth or by whatever. All members of this great nation (The Greatest Nation upon God's Green Earth) are esteemed and are to be treated equal in stature, class, rank, and so forth. They are equal under the law. In practice, of course, that is not always the case, but anyone acting against this principle is acting against the law and should be punished.

All Men are Created Equal

God, the scriptures tell us, is no respecter of persons. All are his children. Each has equal agency to think and act under his own discretion and with whatever ability and judgment he can muster or is blessed with. Everyone is to have equal opportunity limited only by his own initiative or lack thereof. He is free to soar, to cruise, glide, slide and even crash. All men are <u>created</u> equal. And that is where the idea of "equality" should end.

Equality of Outcome

Socialists and people of the left have so misconstrued the meaning of equality as to have rendered it exactly opposite to what the Founders and yes even God intended. Socialism does not allow people to "soar, cruise, glide, slide and crash" at their own discretion. It strictly limits and controls them so as to limit and even eliminate their freedoms altogether and render them slaves to one another.

And with clever use of propaganda, they argue for "fairness, equality, and compassion" to provide reasons for their movement. They, by definition and by reason of necessity, create classes of distinction where certain "elites" are assigned or "elected" to rule over the "leveling" that is required to put into reality the "equality of outcome". And the result is a nation ruled by tyranny and oppression and full of corruption. Yes, all men are equal; it's just that some are more equal than others.

This is not, should not and cannot be the American way. It must be fought at every step. It must be defeated at the voting booth, in schools, churches, social circles and in business. In all walks of life and in all theaters of activity, freedom must be clearly understood, promoted and fiercely defended. For a nation that was created by so much bloodshed and tears for the freedoms that were thus created, to watch as those freedoms are melting, torn away, and destroyed is truly a tragedy of monumental proportion.

America is losing its way by tolerating and permitting this disintegration to continue. WAKE UP AMERICA!

Forced Equality of Outcome is against God's Laws

God said that it is not right that man should be under bondage one to another. When men are forced by threat of law to provide for another the necessities of life, they are in bondage plain and simple. Compassion has nothing to do with it. That is a lie. To force me to have compassion on another to the extent that a third party deems necessary, is to put me under bondage, period. God does not and never has required by force that one have compassion on another. How is that a part of His nature and instruction? Yes, God commands us to have compassion on and care for the poor. But show me where He forces me to comply. Under God's laws, I have the freedom to do so or not to do so. It is my call and my call alone. To force me to have compassion on another is putting me under bondage. How can it be otherwise? For sure, God can and will punish us for breaking or not abiding by His commandments. But that is at His discretion and His alone, not my fellowmen. They have absolutely no right to punish me for my lack of compassion. Rather they should be the ones put in jail and punished for their removing my freedom granted to me by God.

The freedom to my property puts me in charge, not others. I have sole right to enjoy the fruits of my labors and to share them with others to the extent that I choose and at my own discretion. Please respect that and do not use the force of law to strip me of that freedom. I will fight you if you do. That should be the attitude of America. I can be shamed into being compassionate but not forced. Step across the line and you will be facing hostility. Throw them out of office and stop listening to their propaganda. WAKE UP AMERICA!

Who should take care of the Poor?
Not the government, at least not at the federal level. Or probably at any level really. Family, religious, civic, and business associations and organizations, in that order, are more than ready and capable of caring for the poor and downtrodden. They provide the incentives to act with compassion where

people of like-mindedness voluntarily associate and pull together the means to accomplish whatever it takes to care for those in need. Where they are free to do so, this nation has proven without doubt that it has the capacity, the will and the means to provide. And it usually is provided where the recipients can with dignity accept the temporary assistance and be helped to return to productivity and be restored to their own responsibility and self-sufficiency.

The actions of the Federal Government are almost always deleterious to the nation in the long run in these aspects alone: 1) Federal aid renders the people permanently dependent on that aid and that dependency carries through to their children as well. 2) Federal aid destroys the people's incentive to self-sufficiency and responsibility. 3) Federal aid weakens and destroys the people's self-dignity. 4) Federal aid devolves into vote-buying and vast corruption in execution. 5) And Federal aid brings a nation towards bankruptcy as has been the case in Europe and now in America as well because the aid is political without financial responsibility and accountability.

At the level America is now, the entitlements in place cannot be sustained. The national debt, as massive as it has become because revenue is not and cannot be raised high enough to cover entitlement spending and interest on the debt, has grown to the point where the Federal Government has neither the intention nor the capability of ever paying down the debt and reversing the trend. Catastrophe in one form or another is absolutely inevitable. And the reason that is, is because once in place it is impossible to take away entitlements without massive civil unrest or being voted out of office. And that is the truth. That is a subject for another book, however, for sure.

And that is where the rights of property are so negatively impacted. When the fruits of one's labors are more and more confiscated from the producers by force of law and given to the non-producers who receive them as rightful entitlements, the less incentive the producers have to produce. And eventually the demands of the non-producers outstrip the producer's willingness or capability to provide, and a breaking point is reached. Socialism cannot and never will be able to survive in the long run as has been proven every single time it has been tried in history. It is inevitable and that also is the truth.

As Ronald Reagan said many times that freedom and the drive towards it, will always rise to the top and win out in the end. It has to because liberty is a lawful right given to man by his maker and it can only be taken away when men no longer are willing to serve God. For God said, "By the sweat of thy brow shalt thou eat all the days of thy life". Work empowers. Man, only through his industry and thrift, his liberty and freedom, his faith and integrity, does survive and thrive. Without that he is doomed to failure, mediocrity, or bondage.

Property

CHAPTER 5

————●————

PROPERTY RIGHTS - THE ENGINE OF PROSPERITY

Capitalism allows for, fosters, and advances initiative, ingenuity, and creativity. It is the natural way, a natural law native to human existence. It opens the way for humans to implement and provide, to expand and soar, to cherish and reach self-fulfillment. Without individual and corporate property rights, none of this is possible.

Capitalism operates best when left alone, free from government intervention except to protect property rights. And as we have said, with the American Experiment in place, prosperity in America exploded onto the world scene literally changing that world in a most profound way. The standard of living provided by this phenomenon has reached heights never before achieved in the entire world's history. The average standard of living of all Americans has far exceeded even the dreams of kings, magistrates and emperors who have ruled the world in the past.

The Law of Supply and Demand

We describe the process whereby man freely fulfills his material, or human needs and wants, the Free Market. In that free market all men have the liberty to gather and marshal the world's natural resources and combine that with their ingenuity, creativity and human effort (meaning "work") to accomplish all their material wants and needs.

With that liberty and freedom, men can associate and contract with others to maximize the division of labors, determine and accomplish the most efficient and fair distribution of the world's natural resources and the labors of men, thereby fulfilling all men's needs and wants to the maximum limit humanly possible. Men are only limited by their lack of willingness to pitch in and associate and participate in the process. And what is produced and consumed is only limited by men's productivity and other men's wants and needs. These interactions, associations, contracts and all activity in the free market can be compared to the densest spider's cobweb imaginable. The intricate connections are literally infinite in all directions. All boats are lifted together with the tide of prosperity as the free market operates and grows.

The Law of Supply and demand is just that…a natural law. It is the process whereby the free market most efficiently and equitably produces and consumes natural resources, human labors, and the fruits of property rights to the benefit of all mankind. Here is a simple illustration of how that law works:

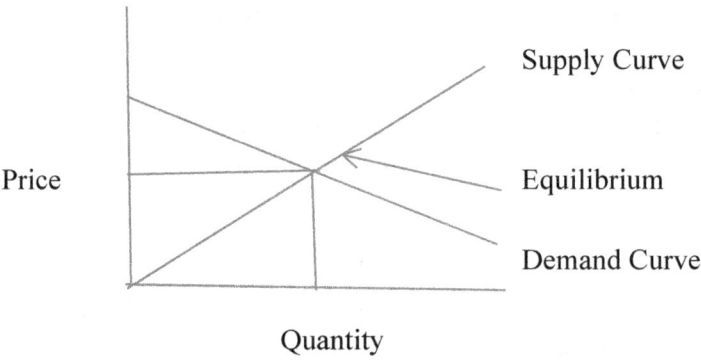

We can take any product, good or service and use as an example, so let's use mousetraps. The horizontal axis represents the quantity of mousetraps produced and the vertical axis represents the cumulative price to consumers that each quantity of mousetraps will cost. That combination produces the upward angled line called the Supply Curve.

The downward angled line represents the Demand Curve created by the market response to all those mousetraps being produced. In other words that line represents to what extent or price, the market is willing to spend to acquire all the mousetraps that it needs or wants. And with each additional mousetrap produced the market is less willing to buy, and can only be coaxed to buy more if the price keeps going down.

At some point, the market becomes saturated to the point where it cannot be coaxed to buy more mousetraps because it has no further need or desire to buy. However, when the demand curve meets the point where the market cannot produce at a lower cost the mousetraps the market is willing to buy, that is the point where productivity stops. That point is where the market will stop producing mousetraps because mousetraps produced at a higher cost than what the market is willing to buy will just sit on producers' shelves. And mousetraps sitting on producers shelves do no one any good. That point is where the Supply Curve and the Demand Curve meet and that point is what is called equilibrium.

Competition drives the price or cost to produce downward thereby flattening the Supply Curve. This in turn, with the lowered price of mousetraps, delivers more mousetraps to the market and more people can enjoy the use of mousetraps because the price just went down, until equilibrium is reached once more and production tapers off at a new level.

There is, of course, much more to it but that is the simplified version of the Law of Supply and Demand. But at least now one can understand how this is a natural law.

Through the Law of Supply & Demand property rights are best apportioned voluntarily among men by contracts and mutual consent, not by legislation or dictate. Market forces instantly direct the flow of goods and services to the areas of greatest need and want of all the people in the market realm. Maximum prosperity is the natural result.

This phenomenon is very clearly demonstrated in the United States in the period between 1929 and 1950. In 1929, America and the rest of the world entered into a devastating economic depression. I will not attempt to describe the reasons except to say that through misguided federal government action, primarily the enactment of the Smoot-Hawley tariff bill, the federal government was the major cause of that devastation.

Unemployment ranged between 14% and 21% for almost 10 years. President Franklyn D. Roosevelt with his army of leftist political tinkerers, enacted through legislation or by executive order, government program after government program to try to prime the economic system to health and productivity. He boasted that through these efforts men could be put back to work doing government jobs, to be restored to dignity and prosperity once more. (People in power in America then were strong followers of Keynesian Economics.) Roosevelt's stated goal was that through his efforts in America there could once more be "...a chicken in every pot and a car in every garage." His efforts may have been more productive had he not got himself caught up in political corruption awarding government money to special interests not related to where the needs were located. But still, in spite of all that Roosevelt did, high unemployment continued unabated and even increased towards the end of the 1920's.

Then along came World War II and America's involvement in 1941. People, including economists and historians originally, mistakenly believed that America's involvement in the war is what turned this Country around economically. Nothing was further from the truth. That there was practically no unemployment was true, but only because all the young went off to war and the remaining people had to be employed in the factories producing war materiel and machinery. No one could buy anything because normal goods and services were not available at prices people could afford because all productivity and resources were being directed to the war effort by government edict. In other words, private property rights were severely restricted because of government mandate and the necessities brought about by the war.

It was not until after the war, and all those fighting men and women returned home, to begin having families again, and suddenly all the personal and normal market needs for housing, clothing, goods and services of every kind, everything that had not been available for purchase for 4-5 years, was in immediate and great demand. All the factories and property of every kind was freely put to work to produce those goods and services and an explosion of prosperity was the result. Once again the free market was unleashed, Roosevelt was dead along with many of his failed programs, and America returned to high employment and productivity.

The free, unfettered market with full private property rights is what provides jobs and maximum prosperity for all. Americans need to stop looking to the federal government to solve economic problems. The less that government does in directing market forces, the more the people prosper. And that is the absolute truth.

Property

CHAPTER 6

————●————

WHAT IS WEALTH

Let's talk about money, first. Basic to human understanding in order to function in the world economic order is to know what wealth is. And of course, everyone learns in school that money is wealth, right? That part is definitely true, that people are taught this popular misunderstanding. Unfortunately, what people are being taught could not be further from the truth.

Money is not wealth. Money represents wealth. It represents the accumulation and result of wealth. It represents the product of wealth. Money is a commodity like oil, wood, tomatoes, or a tool like a hammer, a machine, a pump. Money is only a medium of exchange so that the product of wealth creation can be freely and easily traded between market participants. Money can be used in the creation of more wealth such as putting money to work earning interest. But in that case it merely becomes just another tool.

Popular Myth: There is only a limited amount of money
This myth is regularly taught in schools of America to the everlasting detriment to society. There is only so much money available and the wealthy are hoarding it all, leaving none for the rest of us. The wealthy should be punished through heavy taxation and stripped of their wealth that they undoubtedly extorted from the rest of us, illegally. That there is a fixed sum of money and once the wealthy accumulate their vast portion there is none left for the rest of us; is a bold-faced lie!

Actually, that is two bold-faced lies. One lie is that there is a fixed sum of money available. That particular notion is known as "a zero sum game". Add it all up and there is nothing left, zero. The other lie is that the wealthy are hoarding all the money to the detriment of all others.

If school children were taught the truth about money, wealth and wealth creation they would embrace and emulate the wealthy rather than treat them with scorn, distrust and derision.

Where does Money Come From?
Money comes in many forms and denominations. It is made into paper, coinage, gold, silver, wampum, beads, bales of hay; virtually any commodity of value that the free market agrees to use as a medium of exchange. To exchange what? Exchange productivity or anything of value between market participants. Thus money in reality is nothing more than another commodity or tool.

In every day vernacular and in modern usage, when we speak of money we mean greenbacks and coinage. In America, money is put into circulation through unique machinations involving the Federal Reserve System and the U. S. Treasury, which is a whole other story worthy of another book.

Usually, money needs to be backed up by something else of value to maintain the public trust to continue using that money. Gold and silver historically have been used for that purpose, which help to stabilize the value of money. But, in 1972, President Richard Nixon removed that use in America by the stroke of a pen, to be replaced solely by the "…full faith and credit of the United States." Which in reality is an unknown value but that again is a subject for another book.

In actuality, we apply the law of supply and demand to govern how much money is needed and put into circulation in the marketplace at any given time. Equilibrium is reached when just enough money is added into the market to satisfy the market's demand for it and to where the value of the money remains constant or stable. I should be using the word 'theoretically' because the Federal Reserve System and the US Treasury have so mismanaged the supply of money as to render the dollar anything but stable.

Why has the value of money gone down then? In 1956, when I was pumping gas after school, a gallon of regular cost $0.21, a 7-ounce bottle of Coke $0.05 and a hamburger and chocolate shake cost $0.50. Notwithstanding that there are other factors that determine the price of goods and services, the primary reason that the value of U. S. currency has so drastically depreciated over time is that more money is pumped into the market than is needed (by vast quantities) and the result has been what we call inflation. Inflation is best and simply defined as "too many dollars chasing too few goods."

But, I'm getting off-track here a little bit. The fact is that there is an unlimited supply of money available in the event that the market demands it and will be added into circulation to satiate that demand when needed. So, you see there is no such thing as a "Zero Sum Game". The wealthy can use and control all the money they want and need. More money will be made available when the rest of us need it to purchase all the goods and services we need. No one will be left out if they are still breathing and need to have something to eat, drink, wear, sleep on, or go to school with.

The wealthy can get as rich as they want in America. Their money takes absolutely nothing away from any of the rest of us. Everyone else is as free as another to become as wealthy as they want or can. All the money they need will be made available in the free market as people create the need for it.

What do you mean "…create the need for money"?

Now we're getting to the heart of wealth creation. Wealth is production. It is putting hand to plow, hammer to nail; building, painting, planting, improving, inventing, and developing. Wealth is producing any good or service that another wants or needs which did not exist before. Read that sentence again. There is no limit to wealth creation except that to where the market's demand for any good or service is fully satisfied.

That Bill Gates can make a fabulous fortune inventing and selling a software tool has no bearing on my or your ability to invent and market a better mousetrap, or Steve Jobs' right and ability to invent and market the iphone or ipad. That is the fabulous beauty of the free, capitalist market--producing what others want.

Americans should understand and cherish that freedom. Property rights are at the center of a free market system. Property rights are the engine of prosperity. Wealth is created by the free operation of production. You can become as wealthy as you want. But you must pay the price and cost of putting in the work, the right work. In the real world, and in the final analysis prosperity will not happen if the will to work diminishes and dies. "By the sweat of thy brow shalt thou labor all the days of thy life," is a fact and feature of this mortal life. Work is not punishment, it is a blessing and produces prosperity!

Another Myth: Profit is a dirty word
As a bachelor before getting married, I lived in a house with 4 other fellow roommates, one of which was a dyed-in-the-wool leftist liberal. All of us had jobs and all were college grads. This particular roommate, we'll call him Carl Johnson, had a liberal arts degree with no classes in business, math, economics, or accounting. He was articulate, very opinionated, and grew animated when aroused on the subject of the word profit. His

background, family, education, and experience had all taught him to despise anyone who "took advantage of another" and took a profit from others which he argued was greedy, taking unfair advantage, like stealing. His mind was poisoned to the word and he was blinded by what he had been taught, and many discussions, illustrations and arguments did little to change his thinking.

Let's put things in the simplest of terms. Assume one has a job, any job and at the end of the work period, one is paid his wages for the work he has done. That represents his "income". Subtract from that income all the costs one incurs to perform in that job, including the cost of clothing, transportation to and from work, any special materials, tools, or outside training, and anything else one needs to support and accomplish that job. What is left over is....profit, (Surprise!). If one only received enough remuneration to cover his immediate costs with none left over to go to the movies, take a trip to Disneyland, go out to dinner, or save for retirement, what would be the point in working? Virtually everyone, whether an individual, sole proprietor, corporation large or small, or whatever must make a profit above and beyond one's costs or there would be little or no reason to transact any business.

All for one and one for all (The Three Musketeers' motto) is fairy-tale drivel. It is the empty-headed argument socialist pseudo-intellectual "thinkers" love to sit around and sing praises to. Universities all over the land are full of professors who teach this philosophy which is contrary to natural law; contrary to the notion that all men are free to make their own decisions of how charitable they feel inclined to be. Socialists teach that everyone should perform their work and receive equal pay no matter what they do. It's the equality of outcome "thinking" (or rather non-thinking) again. They fail to understand and realize that the only way all men will come to achieve equality of outcome is when they are all under bondage from someone above them making all the decisions and that is abject slavery. God (including all people on the earth) rejected that notion in our Pre-Mortal existence and God continues to reject that in our mortal existence. All men are free to make as much profit as they legally and honestly can when operating in a free market subject to competition and open market forces, period.

These lies of "equality" are what drive people to demonstrate on Wall Street, at civic centers, businesses; and riot in the face of economic downturns. They are taught to believe that businesses and banks by their very nature are crooked and the causes of these problems. Little do they know that their governments and the people they elect are more to blame than anyone else!

Profits produced at any level allow any entity to freely set aside funds for research and development, purchase plants and equipment for expansion, give to charity to any extent owners please; buy houses, take vacations, save for rainy days, care for elderly parents, or whatever. The list is endless. And every single dollar of profit thus spent results in more jobs, better products, more opportunities, and more prosperity to more and more people. That list is also endless. Profits drive expansion and prosperity. And that is the truth.

Profit is not a dirty word. Teach your children the truth before they get to high school and college where their minds can become contaminated with lies and distortions from men and women out of touch with reality. Unless your children take business, economics or accounting classes you can bet they will be exposed to this socialism contamination.

Property

So, wealth is created by work, productivity, creativity. Productivity, once and perhaps still is, is most highly achieved in this the greatest land in the entire world. Property rights and the rights to the fruits thereof are at the foundation of wealth creation, at the very heart of life, liberty and the pursuit of happiness. Never, ever forget that.

Property

———— ● ————

CHAPTER 7

GREED & CORRUPTION - THE ANTITHESIS OF FREEDOM

There is an Opposition in all Things

A wise and ancient prophet spoke these words of wisdom:

"For it must needs be, that there is an opposition in all things. If not....righteousness could not be brought to pass, neither wickedness, neither holiness nor misery, neither good nor bad. Wherefore, all things must needs be a compound in one; wherefore if it should be one body it must needs remain as dead, having no life neither death, nor corruption nor incorruption, happiness nor misery, neither sense nor insensibility.

"Wherefore, it must needs have been created for a thing of naught; wherefore there would have been no purpose in the end of its creation. Wherefore, this thing must needs destroy the wisdom of God and his eternal purposes, and also the power, and the mercy, and the justice of God.

"And if ye shall say there is no law, ye shall also say there is no sin. If ye shall say there is no sin, ye shall also say there is no righteousness. And if there be no righteousness there be no happiness. And if there be no righteousness nor happiness there be no punishment nor misery. And if these things are not there is no God. And if there is no God we are not, neither the earth; for there could have been no creation of things, neither to act nor to be acted upon; wherefore, all things must have vanished away.

"...but there is a God, and he hath created all things, both the heavens and the earth, and all things that in them are, both things to act and things to be acted upon. And to bring about his eternal purposes...it must needs be that here was an opposition....

"Wherefore, the Lord God gave unto man that he should act for himself. Wherefore, man could not act for himself save it should be that he was enticed by the one or the other."

All men are free to act using their individual agency granted them by their creator. They are free, if permitted by law or lack thereof, to act oppressively against others if they so choose. And those choices are usually a result of the selfish greed in man which has risen beyond the reach of the law, his self-control, or his conscience and good judgment. And therein lies a cancerous culture of greed and corruption.

In most countries of the world and throughout history, where freedom is not found at the level enjoyed in this country by virtue of our Constitution, and where the natural rights of man are trampled upon by tyrannical and dictatorial governments, people have reacted as best they can to obtain what they want and need. As a result, and because in order to do so they have had to operate largely against the laws of such governments, a culture of corruption and lawlessness has virtually permeated these countries and communities.

Here are some true examples of what I mean:

In Russia, a high school teacher announced to her class, students who required a good passing grade in her class in order to gain entry into college, that for them to receive the much-coveted grade, they must each pay her $150 dollars (a sum almost out of the reach of any of them), before the end of the term. At the end everyone agreed, except one person. With that the teacher announced that unless that one person pays, no one else gets the grade.

In Tijuana, Mexico, some U. S. fishermen returning home and almost to the border, made a lane change without using their turn-signal (Note: I wasn't driving!). A local policeman pulled them over, reported their infraction and gave them a choice. They could either pay the policeman $750 right then or they could have their vehicle and all belongs impounded to wait for a court hearing, the judge of which would not be available for at least two days. The travelers bargained him down to $500 and continued on their way knowing the policeman would be pocketing the entire sum (the policeman did not write up a ticket, you see). If they would have waited for the judge, they would have had to pay twice the sum under the table, because...well, that is the way it is in that country.

Greed and corruption are the way of life in most countries. They are found completely throughout society from top to bottom in many countries, and are getting worse as time marches on.

Corruption in America

America is not the country it was 40-50 years ago. Large, historically-respected corporations have imploded because of the graft and corruption of their top officials, owners and managers. Politicians and government officials in record numbers from the federal all the way down to the local level, are being convicted for vice and corruption. Prisons and jails across the land are filled to over-capacity with the lawless. We have witnessed a serious fundamental decline in our standard of living. Many Americans have lost their sense of honor, humility, their respect for life and liberty, and the dedication to personal responsibility that, for 200 years, made our country the greatest hope for mankind.

The decline of our country is a result of major paradigm shifts in so many areas of government, business, religion, education and society in general. It is not the intent of this book to thoroughly treat all these areas. I believe that everyone reading these words senses the truth of what I'm saying, are frustrated by what they sense, and are clueless as to what can be done. But, I would like to cover just a few areas where greed and corruption are having a disastrous effect on America. One might wonder what any of this has to do with property rights, but in my mind it has everything to do with it because of the inter-connection between property rights (including the rights of the fruits thereof); between that and freedom and liberty.

Public Employee Unions
A good place to start in any discussion about corruption in America is with any employee union. Instances of graft and corruption are unlimited in number and scope, covering major industries throughout the land. Many are so corrupt they are entirely controlled by organized crime lords. They enforce their objectives using strong-arm tactics, allowing members no vote or say in how dues are used, and by buying influence illegally, clandestinely, and surreptitiously. They have been responsible for the decline of many industries in America including the automobile, the textile, and the steel industries to name only a few, because they have priced the cost of labor for these industries way beyond world competition. They are the ones most responsible for the decline in U. S. jobs and the flight of businesses to offshore locations. The high taxation and over regulation of American industries are right up there too.

But we're talking about public employee unions who have gained their power through legislation and government edict. In industry, a company brought to the table by unions in collective bargaining, generally have some will and power to resist overly excessive demands, since a company's very survival is on the line. But in the case of public employee unions such as those consisting of government or public school employees things are much different. Federal, state and local governments have neither the will, the interest, the power, nor the backing to stand up to powerful public employee unions, especially when many if not most of these politicians and officials are in their seats of government through the help and support of those very unions.

Resistance to the creation of public employee unions was strong throughout America's history until John F. Kennedy changed all that. Even Franklin Delano Roosevelt, who was the most left-leaning president in history up to that point, recognized that allowing collective bargaining on behalf of government workers was incompatible with a free democratic system of government. In a letter to Luther Steward, president of the National Federation of Federal Employees, August 16, 1937, Roosevelt wrote,

"All Government employees should realize that the process of collective bargaining, as usually understood, cannot be transplanted into the public service. It has its distinct and insurmountable limitations when applied to public personnel management."

Facing tough mid-term elections, the Democratic Party convinced President Kennedy to allow the federal workforce to unionize. By executive order, and not through bi-partisan legislation, he signed on January 17, 1962 Executive Order 10988, permitting federal employees to organize unions and bargain collectively for higher wages and benefits. This set the stage for similar measures in cities and states across the country and led to a transformation of the union workforce.

This represented a major shift in both Democratic Party strategy and a major revolution in American politics. A government union turns the public servant into the public's master. It is a means of using the government's own spending to organize control of that government. And that is exactly what has happened across this great land. *The government, unlike private companies, isn't limited by normal economics because the government controls the monopoly on force and has the power to levy taxes unaffected by immediately-felt consequences to that government.* When the effects are inevitably felt, the guilty politicians are already gone and there is never a direct connection to past bad decisions. The guilty totally escape responsibility for their actions.

The power of unions had long been held in check by market forces. Companies that gave in too much to union demands for higher pay and/or benefits, soon found themselves driven out of the market because of high costs or poor products, and to survive they moved business offshore or collapsed in bankruptcy. Except in cases of government bailout (like GM whose unions are great benefactors to elected politicians), these companies soon went out of business and their union members were left unemployed.

The growth of unions stalled in the 1950's and 1960's, and they began to shrink in the late 1960's. This caused a crisis in the Democratic Party (which is the principal beneficiary of union dues). Something had to be done. Enter John F. Kennedy.

Organizing public employee unions made up of state/federal employees completely eliminated the ability of market forces to temper their power and demands, because taxes (or deficit spending) aren't subject to the demands of consumers. And that is precisely why public employees should have never been allowed to unionize in the first place.

Not surprisingly, following Kennedy's executive order, membership in public employee unions—The American Federation of State, County and Municipal Employees (AFSCME), the Service Employees International Union (SEIU), and the Teachers' National Education Association (NEA)—boomed, better yet, exploded. So did their contributions to liberal, mostly Democratic politicians.

These socialist organizations now had access to power that wasn't limited by market forces. They could control entire generations of politicians, and they did. And still do. From 1989 to 2004, AFSCME was the largest single donor to federal political campaigns in the country. More than 98% of its donations went to Democratic candidates! To see the damage the heavy influence and involvement these unions have had on the nation's states and communities, consider just two examples.

Public Education
The Democrats almost exclusively control all the areas plagued by the worst schools in the United States—the inner city schools of America's big cities. Disrespect for teachers, crime in schools, and failing and falling graduation rates get worse by the year. In the huge, Los Angeles Unified School District alone, the graduation rate is approaching only 50%. Similar, although not as extensive, problems plague the entire State of California, a state which pays out one of the highest amount towards per student education costs in the nation, with the results near the bottom in the country.

A voucher system that would empower parents to send their children to better schools and introduce competition for government funding is a simple and proven way to improve both the results and education's cost-effectiveness. Yet powerful unions consistently unite to defeat almost every effort to allow voucher systems, either through legislation or ballot measures, not only in California but virtually every state of the union.

If the Democratic Party, or the Teachers' Union, were truly interested in the actual well-being of the communities they serve, supporting voucher plans and charter schools is among the first things you'd expect them to pass. But in fact, it is the last thing they would ever voluntarily do. It is the Democratic Party that stands firmly against any significant changes to the public school system—despite its obvious failures—because of lobbying (and political donations) by the NEA.

Among the most important responsibilities of good government, is the duty to protect its citizens from crippling and destructive monopolies. Yet not only has it not done so in the realm of public education, but government is largely responsible for not only the support of but the actual creation of corrupt and crippling monopolies in the field of education in America. Americans are aware of the failures of this system, but they are powerless because of the monopolistic control the teachers' unions have on their governments. That is corruption of the worst sort, aided and supported by taxes from the very Americans who are powerless to stop it.

Public Employee Union Compensation and Retirement Benefits

The second example of the damage done to states, communities and the nation as a whole, caused by unionization of public employees (and the ensuing corruption) is in the effects of exploding compensation and retirement benefits on the financial health of these government entities. The uncontrollable demands of the unions have so markedly increased the compensation and retirement benefits of union members, (i.e. teachers, policemen, firemen, public employees of all kinds), that they have far outstripped those available to the rest of the people in the open market. But, more importantly, these compensations and retirement benefit levels have entirely exceeded the capability of all government entities to fund and pay for them. Almost every retirement benefit fund is bankrupt, unable to sustain even remotely the amount of money required to meet the demands approved by mindless politicians. Approximately 34 of the 50 states in the union, are essentially bankrupt caused in part by the recession, but more especially because of union compensations and retirement benefits exceeding the capability of being funded. And, of course, states are not able, like the federal government, to print money willy nilly to cover their debts. A major catastrophe is soon to hit America as more and more people are told their retirement benefits will not be forthcoming. This catastrophe will be aided by the Federal Government's inevitable inability to fund Social Security and Medicare payments as promised, as well.

Corruption is not Unique to the Democratic Party
Our country's core problems are not found solely in the Democratic Party. There is just as much corruption, if not more, on the Republican side of the aisle. Republican leaders all across the land are being incarcerated for embezzlement, graft, bribery, corruption, and illegal schemes of all kinds. Their votes are being purchased by corporations, unions, and lobbyists just as are Democratic politicians.

Bloomberg news published an article based on confidential sources about how Henry Paulson, the former CEO of Goldman Sachs and the Republican U. S. Treasury Secretary during the financial crisis (which I will get to shortly), held a secret meeting with the top 20 hedge-fund managers in New York City in late July 2008. This was about two weeks after he had testified to Congress that Fannie Mae and Freddie Mac were "well-capitalized."

Yet at that very moment, Fannie and Freddie had billions in losses that they had not as yet revealed to investors--$500 billion in losses at least. In fact, both entities were very much insolvent. And yet, in front of Congress, the U. S. Treasury Secretary was saying just exactly the opposite. But, there is more to the story than just the lying.

After his testimony, only a few short days later, what did Paulson tell those hedge-fund managers? He told them exactly the opposite of what he had publicly told Congress. He told those billionaire investors that Fannie and Freddie were a disaster...That they would require an enormous, multibillion-dollar bailout...The U. S. Government would take them over...And their shareholders would be wiped out. What did this inside information mean to a group of people who represented the financial interests of some of the world's wealthiest folks? These managers had the risk-free ability to make tens of billions of dollars, if not hundreds of billions, by using derivatives to capitalize on what they knew was the imminent collapse of the world's largest mortgage banks. This is the most outrageous example of graft and corruption ever seen on any scale. The story did not come to the public's attention for two years.

One of the investment managers present at this meeting was Steve Rattner, who by that point was already deeply involved in another bit of graft, his efforts to bribe New York state pension-fund managers for large investments into his hedge fund, from which he earned perhaps as much as $100 million. He later settled the charges for a mere $10 million shortly after Andrew Cuomo was elected governor of New York.

The Bloomberg story, about a crooked Treasury secretary handing a room full of crooked billionaires inside information worth billions of dollars…hardly caused a ripple. No actions have been brought against any of them to date, including any from the Department of Justice or the Securities and Exchange Commission. It has simply been ignored.

Corruption at the Highest Levels

At the heart of all corruption lies a simple principle, that of being dishonest. It is a very simple principle, easy to learn, and universal in common understanding, that one should be honest in all one's dealings. What mother or father doesn't strive to teach it; for no one likes to be lied to. The problem with dishonesty is that when people begin to reason falsely that honesty can be or is conditional, then it becomes like a cancer metastasizing throughout the body. It then permeates into the family, the community, the company, the society, the government and everywhere until the whole fabric is eaten through and needs to be discarded, remade, or rebuilt.

When corruption becomes a way of doing business, a way of life, a way of conducting relationships, when it permeates to the top of any system or organization, the entity is doomed and cannot survive for long. It is inevitable. Here are some prime examples taken from the realm of business that demonstrate this point.

WorldCom

Businesses fail for many reasons stemming from normal market forces like competition, or from bad judgment or lack of capital or resources, or from failures due to product obsolescence …of many things. But when the cancer of corruption has spread to the top, the entire business usually implodes...eventually. Take WorldCom for an example.

For a time, WorldCom was the United States' second largest long distance phone company (after AT & T). WorldCom grew largely by aggressively acquiring other telecommunications companies, most notably MCI Communications.

The company began as Long Distance Discount Services, Inc. (LDDS) in 1983. In 1985 LDDS selected Bernard Ebbers to be its CEO. The company went public in 1989 through its first merger and later changed its name to WorldCom. The company's growth under WorldCom was fueled primarily through major, complex acquisitions during the 1990's culminating in the acquisition of MCI in 1998 for $37 billion, making it the largest merger in US history.

CEO Bernard Ebbers became very wealthy from the rising price of his holdings in WorldCom common stock. However, (doesn't that word always grab attention?) in the year 2000, the telecommunications industry entered a downturn and WorldCom's aggressive growth strategy suffered a serious setback and it was forced by the US Justice Department to abandon its proposed merger with Sprint. By that time WorldCom's stock price was declining and Ebbers came under increasing pressure from banks to cover the margin calls on his WorldCom stock that was used to finance his other businesses (timber and yachting, among others).

During 2001, Ebbers persuaded WorldCom's board of directors to provide him corporate loans and guarantees in excess of $400 million to cover his margin calls. The board hoped that the loans would avert the need for Ebbers to sell substantial amounts of his stock, as his doing so would put further downward pressure in the stock's price. However, this strategy ultimately failed and Ebbers was ousted as CEO in April 2002.

Beginning modestly in mid-year 1999 and continuing at an accelerated pace through May 2002, the company (under the direction of Ebbers, Scott Sullivan (CFO), David Myers (Comptroller) and Buford "Buddy" Yates (Director of General Accounting) used fraudulent accounting methods to mask its declining earnings by painting a false picture of financial growth and profitability to prop up the price of WorldCom's stock.

In 2002, a small team of internal auditors at WorldCom worked together, often at night and in secret, to investigate and unearth $3.8 billion in fraud. Shortly thereafter, the company's audit committee and board of directors were notified of the fraud and acted swiftly: Ebbers was ousted, Sullivan was fired, Myers resigned, Arthur Anderson CPA firm (we'll have more to say about them) withdrew its audit opinion for 2001, and the U. S. Securities and Exchange Commission (SEC) launched an investigation into these matters. By the end of 2003, it was estimated that the company's total assets had been inflated by around $11 billion.

On July 21, 2002, WorldCom filed for Chapter 11 bankruptcy protection in the largest such filing in US history at the time (since overtaken by the collapses of both Lehman Brothers and Washington Mutual in a span of eleven days in September 2008, both of which had their fair share of vice and corruption). The SEC and WorldCom reached a deal in which the company agreed to pay a civil penalty of $2.25 billion. WorldCom assets were dispersed by settlement agreements and some were sold off to other companies. Many of the small creditors included former employees, primarily those who were laid off in June

2002 and whose severance and benefits were withheld when the company filed for bankruptcy.

On March 15, 2005 Bernard Ebbers was found guilty of all charges and convicted of fraud, conspiracy and filing false documents with regulators---all related to the $11 billion accounting scandal at the telecommunications company he founded. He was sentenced to prison. Other former WorldCom officials charged with criminal penalties in relation to the company's financial misstatements include former CFO Scott Sullivan (entered a guilty plea to one count each of securities fraud, conspiracy to commit securities fraud, and filing false statements), former comptroller David Myers (pleaded guilty to securities fraud, conspiracy to commit securities fraud, and filing false statements), former accounting director Buford Yates (pleaded guilty to similar charges), and former accounting managers Betty Vinson and Troy Normand (both pleading guilty to conspiracy and securities fraud). On September 26, 2006, Ebbers entered the Federal Bureau of Prisons prison at Oakdale, Louisiana to begin serving his sentence of 25 years.

If it was the nature of these people to lie to such an extent, it makes one wonder to what extent they had lied and cheated in order to build their empire, an empire which turned out to be a house of cards, affecting the lives and fortunes of countless others.

Enron

The Enron scandal, revealed in October 2001, eventually led to the bankruptcy of the Enron Corporation, an American energy company based in Houston, Texas, and the dissolution of Arthur Andersen, which was one of the five largest (and most respected) audit and accountancy partnerships in the world. In addition to being the largest bankruptcy reorganization in

American history at that time, Enron was attributed as the biggest audit failure.

Enron was formed in 1985 by Kenneth Lay after merging Houston Natural Gas and InterNorth. Several years later, when Jeffrey Skilling was hired, he developed a staff of executives that, through the use of accounting loopholes, special purpose entities, and poor financial reporting, were able to hide billions in debt from failed deals and projects. Chief Financial Officer Andrew Fastow and other executives not only misled Enron's board of directors and audit committee on high-risk accounting practices, but also pressured Anderson to ignore the issues.

Shareholders lost nearly $11 billion when Enron's stock price, which hit a high of $90 per share in mid-2000, plummeted to $0.61 by the end of November, 2001. The SEC began an investigation, and rival Houston competitor Dynegy offered to purchase the company at a fire sale price. The deal fell through and on December 2, 2001, Enron filed for bankruptcy. Its $63.4 billion in assets made it the largest corporate bankruptcy in US history until WorldCom's bankruptcy the following year.

Many executives at Enron were indicted and convicted for a variety of charges and were later sentenced to prison. Enron's auditor, Arthur Anderson, was found guilty but by the time the ruling was overturned at the US Supreme Court (for reasons that the jury was not properly instructed), the firm had lost the majority of its customers and had shut down putting 85,000 employees out of work. Employees and shareholders received limited returns in lawsuits, despite losing billions in pensions and stock prices. Many lifetime savings were obliterated and the lives of countless people decimated.

What were these corporate officials and their auditor conspirators guilty of? In a word---dishonesty. They violated their trust in a most reverberating manner and in the broadest outreach possible.

Beginning with Ken Lay, its founder, who built the company from the ground up with complex mergers and acquisitions, the company rose to world dominance. The company owned and operated a variety of assets including gas pipelines, electricity plants, pulp and paper plants, water plants, and broadband services across the globe. Enron was rated the most innovative large company in America in Fortune's Most Admired Companies survey.

However, (there's that word again) Enron's nontransparent financial statements did not clearly depict its operations and finances with shareholders and analysts. In addition, its complex business model and unethical practices required that the company use accounting limitations to misrepresent earnings and modify the balance sheet to portray a favorable depiction of its performance. According to McLean and Elkid in their book *The Smartest Guys in the Room*, "The Enron scandal grew out of a steady accumulation of habits and values and actions that began years before and finally spiraled out of control."

Apparently, from 1997 until its demise, the primary motivations for Enron's accounting and financial transactions seem to have been to keep reported income and reported cash flow up, asset values inflated, and liabilities off the books. The combination of these issues later led to the bankruptcy of the company, spearheaded by the indirect knowledge or direct actions of Lay, Skilling, Fastow and many other executives.

The company was constantly focusing on its stock price. Management was extensively compensated using stock options. This setup of stock option awards caused management to create expectations of rapid growth in efforts to give the appearance of reported earnings to meet Wall Street's expectations. At budget meetings, Skilling would develop target earnings by asking "What earnings do you need to keep our stock price up?" and that number would be used, even if it was not feasible. In 1998, the top 200 highest-paid employees received $193 million from salaries, bonuses, and stock. Two years later, the figure jumped to $1.4 billion.

Fastow and his wife, Lea, both pleaded guilty to charges against them. Fastow was initially charged with 98 counts of fraud, money laundering, insider trading, and conspiracy, among other crimes. He pleaded guilty to two charges of conspiracy and was sentenced to ten years with no parole in a plea bargain to testify against Lay, Skilling, and Causey.

Lay and Skilling went on trial for their part in the Enron scandal in January 2006. The 53–count, 65-page indictment covers a broad range of financial crimes, including bank fraud, making false statements to banks and auditors, securities fraud, wire fraud, money laundering, conspiracy, and insider trading. On May 25, 2006, the jury in the Lay and Skilling trial returned its verdicts. Skilling was convicted of 19 of 28 counts. He was sentenced to 24 years and 4 months in prison.

Lay pleaded not guilty to the eleven criminal charges and claimed that he was misled by those around him. He was convicted on all six counts of securities and wire fraud for which he had been tried and he faced a total sentence of up to 45 years in prison. He died before serving one day of prison time.

Arthur Anderson was charged with and found guilty of obstruction of justice for shredding the thousands of documents and deleting e-mails and company files that tied the firm to its audits of Enron. Its reputation damaged beyond reparation, the company folded, surrendered its CPA license on August 31, 2002, and 85,000 employees (including my son Adam who had just graduated from college working there as an auditor for one month) lost their jobs.

"Oh what a tangled web we weave,
When first we practice to deceive." (Sir Walter Scott, 1771-1832)

The Bernie Madoff Scandal

Return on investment is a term most Americans understand. And stories abound where people have made vast returns after making simple investments. Early investors in many successful business ventures have become wealthy beyond their dreams and some hit the jackpot. But very few people 'hit the jackpot' or win the lottery. And most monopolies are soon enough overtaken by competition, innovation or obsolescence.

But when an enterprise is founded upon fraud and deceit, and corruption is baked into the business model, the results are always devastating to the unwary and trusting. Ponzi schemes, where portions of people's investments are paid back to previous investors represented as profits usually at unheard-of returns, are devastatingly illegal. There have been many such schemes and they seem never-ending, having permeated all types of businesses.

They almost always begin from legitimate business undertakings and where reputations for success are created and fostered. Then, when setbacks occur and the profits can no longer be generated at previous levels, the owners and managers are faced with decisions that turn on moral principles. At first they believe that a little fudging will be only temporary until things return back to normal. Dishonesty which grows into major fraud and corruptions always begins with tiny steps viewed as hardly noticeable and certainly harmful to no one, and will be justified later when success returns. No Ponzi scheme has ever been as large and as devastating as the one woven by Mr. Bernard Madoff except for one perpetrated by the Federal government which I will detail in the following chapter.

Bernard Lawrence "Bernie" Madoff, born April 29, 1938 is a former American businessman, stockbroker, investment advisor, and financier. He is the former non-executive chairman of the NASDAQ stock market, and the admitted operator of a Ponzi scheme that is considered to be the largest financial fraud in U.S. history, so far.

In March 2009, Madoff pleaded guilty to 11 federal felonies and admitted to turning his wealth management business into a massive Ponzi scheme that defrauded thousands of investors out of billions of dollars. Madoff said he began the Ponzi scheme in the early 1990s. However, federal investigators believe the fraud began as early as the 1970s, and those charged with recovering the missing money believe the investment operation may never have been legitimate. The amount missing from client accounts, including fabricated gains, was almost $65 billion. The court-appointed trustee estimated actual losses to investors of $18 billion. On June 29, 2009, Madoff was sentenced to 150 years in prison, the maximum allowed.

On December 10, 2008, Madoff's sons told authorities that their father had confessed to them that the asset management unit of his firm was a massive Ponzi scheme, and quoted him as describing it as "one big lie."

Madoff insisted he was solely responsible for the fraud. He did not plea bargain with the government. Rather, he pleaded guilty to all charges. It has been speculated that Madoff pleaded guilty because he refused to cooperate with the authorities in order to avoid naming any associates and conspirators who were involved with him in the Ponzi scheme.

In his plea allocution, Madoff stated he began his Ponzi scheme in 1991. He admitted he had never made any legitimate investments with his clients' money during this time. Instead, he said, he simply deposited the money into his personal business account at Chase Manhattan Bank. When his customers asked for withdrawals, he paid them out of the Chase account—a classic "robbing Peter to pay Paul" scenario. Chase and its successor, JPMorgan Chase, may have earned as much as $483 million from his bank account. He was committed to satisfying his clients' expectations of high returns, despite an economic recession. He admitted to false trading activities masked by foreign transfers and false SEC filings. He stated that he always intended to resume legitimate trading activity, but it proved "difficult, and ultimately impossible" to reconcile his client accounts. In the end, Madoff said, he realized that his scam would eventually be exposed.

To be sure, many in his organizations knew and participated in the scheme(s), including family members who made fabulous sums in the process. And, although many investors were innocent and unwary losers, many also knew that the returns were mathematically unsustainable and were merely gambling that they could bow out before the whole thing collapsed, just as participants in a chain letter scheme know that eventually it will play out and collapse but the losses will be borne by others and that's somehow OK. After all, life is a gamble anyway, right?

America's 2008 Financial Meltdown - Caused by Government

Ever the cause of so much economic and financial distress, the US Federal Government rarely is shown to be the culprit when all cards are played. Oh to be sure, it comes under much criticism...when more socialism is called for. But the mainstream media rarely delves into governmental systemic corruption and mismanagement on its own even when it occurs at unprecedented levels; and most people are left in the dark because of that dereliction.

Consider the case of Fannie Mae and Freddie Mac and their roles in the great financial meltdown which erupted in 2008. In that year the huge real estate boom and subsequent prosperity bubble came to an abrupt end. The mortgage financial structure, a whole host of banks around the world, Wall Street stock, and the values of every home in the country collapsed and/or plummeted. Businesses failed, enterprises were thrown out of existence, and unemployment soared to 12-14% to remain there for 5 years and still has not come down at this writing. Every investor who bought mortgage-based bonds has experienced major losses and the economies all around the world have been seriously affected. Today, over 40% of all homes in the US are under water with values below their mortgages. Foreclosures have been at astronomically high levels for these five years and are not expected to turn back down for at least another 4 years. On average 1 in 7 homes in this country is in some stage of foreclosure and in some areas it rises to 1 in 4.

What caused this to happen? Who or what is at fault? Who can be blamed and how do we hold them accountable? Was this just another business cycle coming to an end? The US media has found many to share in the blame including Wall Street, banks, greedy mortgage brokers, a failed financial system using sophisticated and complicated derivative instruments, insurance schemes and more, many of whom were bailed out by the Fed.

But precious few fingers have been pointed in the direction of Congress or the government where the blame is most deserved.

Fannie Mae and Freddie Mac were first created as quasi-businesses with strong ties to the Federal government. Their top managers are appointed by Congress and policies are heavily influenced and guided the same way. Their purpose was to become the major player in buying up real estate mortgages created in the US marketplace, setting basic guidelines for the mortgage industry, securely backed by the full faith and credit of the US government. Fannie Mae mortgage guidelines were the industry standard and for a time they were proven to be failsafe and provided stability and safety to the industry. At their peak, these two organizations purchased and held over 50% of all US mortgages. Through their policies and guidelines and by virtue of their enormous size and influence they became the flagships around the world in mortgage-backed securities. That and because the US government provided the risk protection needed, they were the financial backbone to the whole real estate financial world.

1999, the beginning of the Economic Boom
Fannie was deeply involved in the politically instigated move to lower lending requirements in the name of helping "disadvantaged" groups. In September 1999, the *New York Times* reported that Fannie Mae was easing credit requirements on the mortgages it bought from banks. The initiative, the *Times* said, would encourage banks "to extend home mortgages to individuals whose credit is generally not good enough to qualify for conventional loans."

Fannie Mae had been under heavy pressure from the Clinton Administration to expand mortgage loans among low and moderate income people. One of the program's goals was to increase the number of minority and low-income homeowners who tended to have worse credit ratings and lower income ratios than non-Hispanic Whites. Almost prophetically the *Times* article went on to say,

"In moving, even tentatively, into this new area of lending, Fannie Mae is taking on significantly more risk, which may not pose any difficulties during flush economic times. But the government-subsidized corporation may run into trouble in an economic downturn, prompting a government rescue similar to that of the savings and loan industry in the 1980's"

And brother did that ever come to pass.

Paradigm Shift in Mortgage Lending

This proved to be the paradigm shift that started the real estate boom and which later caused its collapse. Pressured by Congress, particularly the Democratic Party but also supported by many prominent Republicans including President George W. Bush; and more specifically pressured by Democratic Senator Christopher Dodd and Democratic Congressman Barney Frank who had direct oversight of the two entities; and pressured by minority interests across the broad spectrum of America, all crying to increase the blessings of home ownership to all those poor, unfortunate souls who have been left out, Fannie and Freddie delivered.

By reducing acceptable credit scores, income levels, down payments needed, and borrower safety reserve requirements, Fannie and Freddie were responsible for the wave of new mortgage instruments loosely called "sub-prime loans." They began to purchase in unprecedented volumes variable rate loans with short term fuses and rapidly escalating interest rates under the new qualification guidelines.

At the center of this new wave of pressure was Senator Chris Dodd who was the general chairman of the Democratic National Committee from 1995 to 1997, and Chairman of the powerful Senate Banking Committee, and Congressman Barney Frank who later served as Chairman of the Congressional Banking Committee. In their key roles in the government, these men had a most powerful influence over Fannie and Freddie. And it was mainly from them that this new philosophy of spreading the blessings of home ownership to those currently being left out was put into true effect.

At first, they were met with much resistance from people within Fannie Mae and Freddie Mac because achieving their goals meant going against the proven wisdom of the mortgage industry from literally millions and millions of loans which had shaped the industry standards developed by Fannie Mae. Experience told the industry experts what would happen if allowable credit scores were lowered, allowable income ratios relaxed, and other important standards relaxed. Fannie and Freddie initially resisted this pressure.

In 1999 President Bill Clinton appointed Franklin D. Raines as CEO of the then rather obscure but powerful Fannie Mae. Raines immediately went to work lobbying Congress for less regulation and more "flexibility" in creating the massive dodgy-loan portfolio of under-qualified home loans to fellow minorities which would continue to grow under the encouragement of Congressman Barney Frank heading up the House Financial Services Committee (which has a key oversight over both Fannie and Freddie).

In addition, Mr. Raines instituted a massive pay and bonus incentive program for himself and top executives to reward (and provide the incentive for) the subsequent huge build-up of weak, subprime and Alt-A loans that were purchased and guaranteed by Fannie (i.e. the Federal government). It was not until after that, in the early 2000's that Fannie and Freddie grew to gargantuan size buying up over 50% of all loans (and in the end, 2007 and 2008, buying up 75% of all new subprime loans).

That Mr. Raines, subsequently forced to resign amid a giant scandalous accounting nightmare he oversaw whereby Fannie overstated its earnings by over $10 billion so he and other executives could "earn" higher bonuses and salaries, is another story entirely. He took "early" retirement and got a golden parachute worth over $250 million in cash and "benefits." He was sued by the government, defended by Fannie at taxpayer's expense to the tune of $160 million. He settled and agreed to pay $24.7 million. The court also ordered him to return $50 million he received in bonuses based on the miss-stated profits. The government noted that "The 101 charges reveal how those individuals improperly manipulated earnings to maximize their bonuses, while knowingly neglecting accounting systems and internal controls, misapplying over twenty accounting principles and misleading the regulator and the public."

Another key individual in this whole shady matter was Mr. Tim Howard who was the Chief Financial Officer of Fannie Mae. Howard was a strong internal proponent of using accounting "strategies" that would ensure a "stable pattern of earnings" at Fannie. Translation—he was cooking the books. The government investigation determined that, "Chief Financial Officer, Tim Howard, failed to provide adequate oversight to key control and reporting functions with Fannie Mae." Howard shared in the $31.4 million settlement. He too resigned under pressure and his golden parachute is estimated to be over $20 million.

These key individuals and several others not mentioned here should be serving prison terms like Ken Lay and Bernie

Madoff. Instead they are scot-free and rumored to be serving in the Obama Administration as economic "advisors."

More Government Meddling

In addition to Fannie's and Freddie's disastrous involvement in the mortgage industry and their flagship roles, both political parties (but more particularly the Democratic Party), through governmental housing agencies and bank regulatory agencies, began putting huge pressure on banks and mortgage bankers to lower credit standards so that low-income and minorities could thereby participate in the blessings of home ownership. Quotas were established and enforced and contributed greatly to the insanity that enveloped the real estate mortgage industry. And in the frenzy to satisfy the vastly increased demand for real estate loans, banks and mortgage brokers, to their discredit, became embroiled in fraudulent methods to increase their earnings in this new-found prosperity. And why not since the federal government through its backing of Fannie and Freddie was absorbing all the risk anyway.

Fannie and Freddie continued to build up ever-riskier obligations. Creative financing was encouraged such as no-down loans, no-doc loans, 125% loan-to-value loans, and 2-3 year interest-only loans with 2-3 year 'teaser rates' well below market.

These latter loans were potential time-bombs because after the teaser-rates expired in 2-3 years, 3 things would happen: 1) payments would have to be increased to include principle as well as interest, 2) amortization of the loan would be shortened by 2-3 years making the resulting payment much higher than a normal 30 year loan, and 3) the interest rate would shift to a market rate usually well above the teaser rate.

All of these could put the resulting payments way above what the borrower could handle and above what he had originally been qualified for. But never mind, since real estate values were soaring these interest-only loans could easily be refinanced to create yet another subprime loan. And of course, refinancing brought more fee revenues to the mortgage industry, don't you know! All went well....for a time.

So What Caused the Economic Boom?

It does not take a nuclear scientist to determine what happened. Normally, the supply and demand for housing is based almost entirely on population trends, except in minor cases of anomaly such as when Taiwanese cash flowed into the US to buy real estate when the threat of Chinese takeover loomed.

Now you had an enormous surge in real estate loan demand based on the forgoing insanity. Home builders could not keep up. Real estate values soared (and went through the roof). Home values were increasing at rates of 15-20% annually. And soon, the industry began to believe that that would be the new norm and acted accordingly. Banks and mortgage lenders, Fannie and Freddie, mortgage investors, Congress, politicians, Wall Street, speculators and people in general, never seemed worried that the bubble would ever burst.

With constantly rising home values and America's proclivity to increase debt and spend beyond their means, people began using their new-found home equities to spend, spend and spend some more. Financing was easy, interest rates were low (also encouraged by the Fed), values were always growing to replenish the equities which were being used to purchase consumer goods and services. And consumption became the major force driving the economy.

And that is what caused the economic boom of the period between the late 1990's and early 2000's culminating in late 2007 and early 2008.

And What Caused the Economic Bust?

No one living today anywhere in the free world is unaware of the extremely difficult economic times that are upon us. Untold millions of jobs have been lost; real estate values have plummeted (and are still not stabilized as yet because of so many non-paying mortgages left to be foreclosed on); government tax revenues have shrunk considerably; and businesses have not only suffered huge reductions but many have simply closed down adding to the high unemployment; and the list of difficulties seems endless.

So what happened? Why did this happen? The government, politicians and the main-stream media have attempted to lay the blame on "Wall Street", greedy and out-of-control banks, the lack of government regulation, unethical mortgage and real estate industries, the rich, and everyone else except where it is most deserving… the government and politicians themselves.

What really happened to cause the bust can be explained in simple Econ 101 terms by referring again to the law of supply and demand. When the government-inspired "let's spread the blessings of home ownership to all those low-income and minority people" paper moon took hold, it immediately unleashed a huge addition to the overall demand for housing. And, as has been explained, enter the economic boom and the unsustainable notion that not only are good times here but the end is nowhere in sight…"let's keep spending, don't worry because we can always refinance" with higher home values.

Well, the end did finally arrive as everyone now knows. Supply of homes eventually met demand and demand no longer soared above supply. Home values stopped rising. And with it the propensity to keep refinancing disappeared into thin air because new equities were no longer able to feed the economic frenzy. Business tapered off because the demand for goods and services began to plummet. People were laid off and could no longer pay for their high mortgages. Those "precious new home owner"' the ones who were shoehorned into subprime mortgages, the ones targeted by government to be the recipients of the blessings of home ownership previously denied them, were the first to fail in their mortgage payments. And because they were the ones who had lower-than-proven standards of creditworthiness, income levels, and propensities to be economically responsible, they failed in record numbers. Speculators, who invariably add upward demand pressures when values are soaring (speculation is a phenomenon which occurs in anything where values are soaring for any reason), were among the first to drop out of the market adding to the downturn. The misery worsened when the short fuses on the subprime teaser-rate loans expired and could no longer be refinanced. Serious trouble was on the horizon. And, over time, the sickness has spread to the general population, where job losses have rendered even the vast middleclass the inability to keep up their mortgage payments and the values of their homes became submerged under water and continue to remain so even 6 years after the downturn began.

And don't get your hopes up too soon, all you homeowners. Good times (and rising real estate values) are not likely to return until the population growth naturally absorbs the massive oversupply of housing created because of the unnatural rise in demand caused by empty-headed politicians and regulators. And that is not likely to occur soon since the US birthrate is hovering around 2.1, (barely above keeping even), and the population bubble created after WWII is now moving into retirement (and taking up permanent residence in the nation's graveyards). So don't count on that housing absorption occurring any time soon.

And now you know why politicians on both sides of the aisle are beginning to favor illegal immigration as population growth will be necessary to overcome our economic difficulties. Never mind, no worries that this influx is from the bottom of the barrel with people of low educations, low skills, and low propensities for upward mobility, entering the job market at the lowest possible income levels, the people of which send a majority of their earnings back to the countries of their origin and whose allegiance remains with those mother countries. No worries there, right?

CHAPTER 8

SOCIAL SECURITY & MEDICARE
The Greatest Ponzi Schemes of all Time

If the title of this next chapter is enough of a turnoff that you will not read on, then you should realize your head is buried in the sand and you are indeed—afraid of the truth. In time, it will matter to every American because every American will be adversely affected by the result of this the greatest sham ever to be perpetrated on this great nation.

That the truth about Social Security and Medicare is withheld from the public by the main stream media and politicians was made ever so evident in the 2012 Presidential Primary election campaigning. When Governor Rick Perry attacked the federal Social Security program by calling it (what it really is) nothing more than a giant Ponzi scheme he was immediately and viciously attacked by both the media and politicians from both sides. A firestorm of criticism erupted from talking heads at CNBC, ABC and *The New York Times,* the Democratic Party and from Republicans as well.

Mitt Romney, sensing an opportunity to halt Perry's surge in the polls, went even further than he did on the debate stage, asserting in blunt terms that the new frontrunner had rendered himself unelectable and that his nomination could lead to a 2012 GOP wipe-out.

"If we nominate someone who the Democrats could correctly characterize as being against Social Security we would be obliterated as a party," the former Massachusetts governor said without prompting in an afternoon appearance on Sean Hannity's radio show.

Ironically, Romney was right in saying that, even though there is not a politician in America that doesn't know that Social Security, Medicare and all other entitlement programs eventually will bankrupt this nation because they are virtually and inescapably unsustainable. He was right because there is also not a single politician willing or able to do anything about it.

Social Security and Medicare largely are brainchildren of the Socialistic Left but which are avidly supported by all politicians because so many Americans have become dependent upon them. These programs are so entrenched that they will never be modified enough to render them fiscally survivable. And that is the absolute truth.

Social Security came into being during Franklin Roosevelt's time in office and was developed and sold to the American people. Americans were initially skeptical of yet another government program forcing everyone to pay into it and forcing all employers to carry it out through payroll deductions. Their reluctance was eventually overcome by the false notion that the government would safely take care of their "investments into their retirements" and have the money ready for them when they needed it in retirement. It was falsely implied that the government would treat their investment like any other annuity, investing or saving the funds and have enough buildup in the giant fund to cover the drawdowns needed later. It was represented to be a program like any other retirement fund in the business world. That was a total sham.

Shortly after the program was underway and the government needed additional revenues that were unavailable from taxation, all the moneys were drawn out of the "retirement fund" and replaced by government IOU's. And so the "fund" is now nothing more than a bunch of government IOU's---lots of

IOU's. There was never an ounce of effort to save that money or invest it for future growth as originally promised. It became nothing more than a scam to be covered by future taxation of future taxpayers. And what is that if not a Ponzi scheme.

In fact the whole scheme was nothing more than another taxation program to provide additional revenues for the government's general fund, which could not be provided by mutually agreed upon tax legislation. This was a scheme which could never be abolished by future meddlesome conservative politicians because the stream of future revenues needed to fund the retirement payments were guaranteed by the government's promise to return those funds in the sometime distant future. And the scheme was guaranteed also because people would consider a reduction in their future retirement benefits a theft of the highest order. And that is precisely what FDR wanted, a taxation program that could never be reversed in the future. Never mind that it was built on a bold-faced massive lie, because they never intended to treat the money like an ordinary pension fund in the first place.

There is no need to argue what their original intentions were anyway. That it is, in reality, a huge Ponzi scheme cannot be denied by any rational human being still capable of breathing. A Ponzi scheme is defined as taking someone's money who thinks he is making an investment and using that money to pay out to previous investors a supposed return on their investments period. And, like all Ponzi schemes, eventually the whole thing will collapse because future revenues at some point will not be enough to pay back all previous investors, who will be left holding the empty bag.

And yet the government still masquerades the Social Security program as a "fund." But the end is clearly coming into view right now. The "fund" is becoming depleted now that deductions from current incomes are not enough to cover current retirees' demands and fulfill "entitlements" promised. And with the huge baby boomer population just beginning to enter retirement, the rate in which the federal government is going to have to feed cash into social security payments is going to explode into the stratosphere. And like all entitlement programs (also unsustainable) the government is going to have to make one of two choices. One, raise taxes or two, deficit spend…meaning print money.

And the reason these programs, mainly Social Security and Medicare, are now unsustainable is from one simple fact. The demands and required outlays have become so great that they cannot be paid for through reasonable taxation levels. And the baby boomers have barely begun retiring.

Social Security and Medicare after shedding the light of reality are nothing more than complete shams. They are mechanisms for the government to raise uncontrollable taxes from current taxpayers on the promise that those current taxpayers will receive some future benefits which actually will be paid for by future taxpayers. If these programs had been presented to American voters with any degree of truth as to this reality, what American voter would have agreed to that? Who in his right mind would have wished that on his children or grandchildren?

In the next chapter we'll discuss what these entitlement programs have done to America.

CHAPTER 9

———————●———————

ENTITLEMENTS ARE BURYING AMERICA

Provide for the Common Defense

Providing for the common defense is prescribed in the Constitution as the primary responsibility of the Federal Government. And in performing that responsibility when duty called, the government has been forced to raise cash to fight and put forces in place. In early American history it did that by not only raising taxes, of course, but more importantly by borrowing directly from foreign governments, large corporations and even individual people. As a child during WWII, I remember seeing big colorful posters at the post office and on city main streets, depicting Uncle Sam with his hand humbly held out urging people to "Support our troops, Buy American Liberty Bonds". That was the beginning of our huge National Debt. And in early times, the notion was to pay off that debt…and for a time it was paid off. But eventually, it wasn't.

Provide for the General Welfare

Here is the Preamble to the US Constitution:

*"**We the People** of the United States, in Order to form a more perfect Union, establish Justice, insure domestic Tranquility, provide for the common defence (sic), promote the general Welfare, and secure the Blessings of Liberty to ourselves and our Posterity, do ordain and establish this Constitution for the United States of America."*

Two phrases bear looking into; 'Provide for the common defense', and 'Promote the general welfare'. There is a distinct difference between the meanings of the words "provide" and "promote". Provide means actually doing, supplying or furnishing something. Promote means encouraging, or working actively to stir up interest but not actually supplying something. With the growth of Progressivism and modern Liberalism, 'Promote" in the Preamble has come to mean 'Provide'.

Progressivism had its proponents in America as early as the nation's founding when Alexander Hamilton and others were on the "opposite side of the aisle" to Thomas Jefferson, Samuel and John Adams. In those days Hamilton's ideas took a back seat to Jefferson's, Madison's, Adam's and others'.

However, beginning with Theodore Roosevelt and especially Woodrow Wilson the notions of government involvement in the lives of the people began a paradigm shift. In their administrations Progressivism and Modern Liberalism took root and began to take this nation into the realm of entitlements for the people. At first they were resisted. In fact, Wilson, Hoover and especially FDR vigorously campaigned against preceding administrations because they had strayed away from Constitutional principles of liberty, etc. But after arriving in office they continued doing what they had criticized their predecessors of doing and in progressively more and more ways.

FDR, however, especially in his third and fourth terms, because of the deleterious effects of the massive depression, actively campaigned for entitlement programs selling the American voters that they were "rights" of the people. Providing "A chicken in every pot, and a car in every garage" became his holy call to duty. It was during his time that the American Propaganda Machine began to flourish.

But it was in Wilson's time that the propaganda took root. A prerequisite for national progress, Wilson believed, was that the founding be understood in its proper historical context. The principles of the founding, in spite of their claims of universality, were intended to deal with the unique circumstances of that day, he argued. Wilson looked instead to what he believed to be the democratic spirit of the founding--- one that established national government as a work-in-progress, a government that would require continual adjustment to historical circumstances as it tried to fulfill the broad democratic vision of the founders. In other words, in Wilson's mind the constitution was a "living" document and should be changed with the times. During the founding the country was an agrarian society, but as modern times came upon us, things changed and so should the Constitution, Wilson and thinkers of the day believed.

And so "change" became the watchword of the day and still continues as we well know. What started out as slight drifts has now become a stampede towards socialism and the abrogation of liberty and property rights. The rich and successful people are derided and scorned by politicians and the media and portrayed as greedy and full of selfishness. They hoard all the money leaving little, less and none for the 99, it is claimed. People should not be entitled to more when the low-income sector and the poor are left without. They have "rights" that are not being met, and so it is the government's duty and responsibility to provide.

FDR certainly did his part. In the face of economic hard times he raised taxes and increased debt and directed those funds to states and areas who supported his re-elections and other fellow Democrats in the name of "helping" America regain prosperity. Instead his programs prolonged the Depression and indeed during his four-term administration unemployment not only did not improve but worsened.

Nevertheless the die was cast and the propaganda ensued. Poverty had to be stamped out, the poor and downtrodden had to be supported, welfare programs rose and became entrenched. As politicians fought over whether to move in the direction of progressivism or conservatism the arguments turned on whether we should spend on "guns or butter". Should Congress spend more on military and defense (guns) or on helping the poor (butter)? The progressives won out and eventually, for the first time, entitlement spending surpassed defense spending and soon soared way past.

John F. Kennedy, born into a rich family whose father built an empire bootlegging liquor from Canada and Mexico during prohibition days, took up the cross. During his campaign he toured low-income areas in the East at great media fanfare in his quest to convince Americans that poverty was rampant in America and more should be done to eliminate it. He rode the fanfare into office. But it was not until his successor, Lyndon Johnson, came to power that entitlement programs began to choke America.

Johnson declared "War on Poverty" and in spite of inheriting the war in Viet Nam, a war he largely ignored and had no intention of winning, he focused instead on his other war. Medicare was conceived and passed and as always it was intended to be self-sustaining and again was sold on the same claims that Social Security was based on…that the funds forcibly taken from taxpayers would be held in trust for later times when needed. But instead it has become an even bigger Ponzi scheme than its predecessor, the funds added into the general fund the instant they are received.

Welfare programs designed to "help" the poor instead destroyed the incentive to marry as funds were directed heavily to unmarried women with children---the more children they had the more they could get. The more people could claim the need for whatever--- lack of food, lack of lunch money, lack of rent money, lack of insurance, general lack of money, lack of almost anything, the government has tried to come to the rescue. Welfare is treated much like a business in a way, its services advertised and promoted in the same way as any product. For six years, while I had my mortgage business (yes during the boom subprime loan days), my desk faced outward so that I could see all the clientele who came to the market next door which only catered to those holding food stamps. The majority of the people was very well dressed and drove large SUVs and late model cars. Signs of poverty were seldom evident.

Immigrants who enter this country illegally and who do not pay "their fair share" of taxes, or any taxes more likely, participate freely in welfare and medical services offered free to the public, obtain free schooling and countless "free" goods and services provided by government largesse.

Yet in spite of all this spending to alleviate the angst, the poor are still among us and indeed the low-income sector has increased over time. Not only has the government destroyed the will to work and the incentive to be self-sustaining for many people, but it has made a vast sector of America totally dependent on government welfare and handouts. Succeeding generations born into welfare homes are not likely to rise out of poverty but will only perpetuate them and dependency will continue to be increased.

The rise in entitlement programs during the 60's, 70's and 80's was partially overshadowed by the burgeoning baby boomers moving into productive jobs. Incomes were rising, unemployment was low, more homes were needed to house the growing numbers of families and so on. Tax revenues flowed. And then the boom times from the subprime mortgage morass continued the "prosperity."

But economic prosperity and growth are not likely to be returning any time soon. Real estate values will remain submerged for some time as the nation works its way out of the disaster. And, more importantly, baby boomers will be retiring in vast numbers and the same effect they had on booming economic times in the past will occur only in reverse as they stop being wealth producers and become dependent on social security, Medicare, and even welfare.

The Bailout Syndrome-
Business Joins the Entitlement Game

During Wilson's, Hoover's and more importantly FDR's administrations, bailouts designed for individuals fell directly to the benefit of America's corporations, ostensibly to provide jobs and prevent collapses. But nevertheless, the die was cast. The US Government proclaimed loudly to the world that it was now prepared to assume business risk that in a free market economy such as was designed and envisioned by the Founders, was to be shouldered by the private sector.

The important word here is "risk.". In any business venture, one gambles that the future result will be worth the invested effort. It is a gamble because no one really knows what the future will bring. When one gambles with his own savings and resources on the line, one is far more cautious to avoid disaster and failure. Failure in business results in lessons learned and one, or someone else, rebuilds and redirects assets and resources in a more productive course. But if one is assured that someone else, like the government, will be ready to absorb any losses, then caution can be thrown to the wind. One cannot always be certain the government will bail you out and so political connections can improve the likelihood. And politicians are quite ready to serve with their hands out.

The inside stories are most often withheld from public view. In very large cases, however, the light of day is shed on the bailouts and Congress passes legislation to accomplish them, almost always defended by the airy notion that "they are too big to fail". The shifting of business risk to the Federal Government has now reached unprecedented new heights in alarmingly warp speed. Here is a short list illustrating the growing problem.

Who	Year	What Happened	Cost in 2008 U.S. Dollars
Penn Central Railroad	1971	In May 1970, Penn Central Railroad, then on the verge of bankruptcy, appealed to the Federal Reserve for aid on the grounds that it provided crucial national defense transportation services. The Nixon administration and the Federal Reserve supported providing financial assistance to Penn Central, but Congress refused to adopt the measure. Penn Central declared bankruptcy on June 21, 1970, which freed the corporation from its commercial paper obligations. To counteract the devastating ripple effects to the money market, the Federal Reserve Board told commercial banks it would provide the reserves needed to allow them to meet the credit needs of their customers.	$3.2 billion
Lockheed	1974	In the first five months of 1974 the bank lost $63.6 million. The Federal Reserve stepped in with a loan of $1.75 billion.	$7.8 billion
New York City	1975	During the 1970s, New York City became over-extended and entered a period of financial crisis. In 1975 President Ford signed the New York City Seasonal Financing Act, which released $2.3 billion in loans to the city.	$9.4 billion

Chrysler	1980	In 1979 Chrysler suffered a loss of $1.1 billion. That year the corporation requested aid from the government. In 1980 the Chrysler Loan Guarantee Act was passed, which provided $1.5 billion in loans to rescue Chrysler from insolvency. In addition, the government's aid was to be matched by U.S. and foreign banks.	$4.0 billion
Continental Bank	1984	Then the nation's eighth largest bank, Continental Illinois had suffered significant losses after purchasing $1 billion in energy loans from the failed Penn Square Bank of Oklahoma. The FDIC and Federal Reserve devised a plan to rescue the bank that included replacing the bank's top executives.	$9.5 billion
Savings & Loans	1989	After the widespread failure of savings and loan institutions, President George H. W. Bush signed and Congress enacted the Financial Institutions Reform Recovery and Enforcement Act in 1989.	$293.3 billion
Airline Industry	2001	The terrorist attacks of September 11 crippled an already financially troubled industry. To bail out the airlines, President Bush signed into law the Air Transportation Safety and Stabilization Act, which compensated airlines for the mandatory grounding of aircraft after the attacks. The act released $5 billion in compensation and an additional $10 billion in loan guarantees or other federal credit instruments.	$18.6 billion
Bear Stearns	2008	JP Morgan Chase and the federal government bailed out Bear Stearns when the financial giant neared collapse. JP Morgan purchased Bear Stearns for $236 million; the Federal Reserve provided a $30 billion credit line to ensure the sale could move forward.	$30 billion

Fannie Mae & Freddie Mac	2008	On Sep. 7, 2008, Fannie and Freddie were essentially nationalized: placed under the conservatorship of the Federal Housing Finance Agency. Under the terms of the rescue, the Treasury has invested billions to cover the companies' losses. Initially, Treasury Secretary Hank Paulson put a ceiling of $100 billion for investments in each company. In February, Tim Geithner raised it to $200 billion. The money was authorized by the Housing and Economic Recovery Act of 2008.	$400 billion
American International Group (A.I.G.)	2008	On four separate occasions, the government has offered aid to AIG to keep it from collapsing, rising from an initial $85 billion credit line from the Federal Reserve to a combined $180 billion effort between the Treasury ($70 billion) and Fed ($110 billion). ($40 billion of the Treasury's commitment is also included in the TARP total.)	$180 billion
Auto Industry	2008	In late September 2008, Congress approved a more than $630 billion spending bill, which included a measure for $25 billion in loans to the auto industry. These low-interest loans are intended to aid the industry in its push to build more fuel-efficient, environmentally-friendly vehicles. The Detroit 3 -- General Motors, Ford and Chrysler -- will be the primary beneficiaries.	$25 billion
Troubled Asset Relief Program	2008	In October 2008, Congress passed the Emergency Economic Stabilization Act, which authorized the Treasury Department to spend $700 billion to combat the financial crisis. Treasury has been doling out the money via an alphabet soup of different programs. Here's the running tally of companies getting TARP funds.	$700 billion

Citigroup	2008	Citigroup received a $25 billion investment through the TARP in October and another $20 billion in November. (That $45 billion is also included in the TARP total.) Additional aid has come in the form of government guarantees to limit losses from a $301 billion pool of toxic assets. In addition to the Treasury's $5 billion commitment, the FDIC has committed $10 billion and the Federal Reserve up to about $220 billion.	$280 billion
Bank of America	2009	Bank of America has received $45 billion through the TARP, which includes $10 billion originally meant for Merrill Lynch. (That $45 billion is also included in the TARP total.) In addition, the government has made guarantees to limit losses from a $118 billion pool of troubled assets. In addition to the Treasury's $7.5 billion commitment, the FDIC has committed $2.5 billion and the Federal Reserve up to $87.2 billion.	$142.2 billion

To the above list we should add "Obama Care" which was signed into law in 2010. This program ensures by force of law the never-before requirement that all Americans purchase health insurance whether they want to or not. The resulting cost increase to the Government will grow to absorb a vast portion of GDP, and the Government will assume the role of determining who will get health care and by how much. That right and responsibility, in time, will no longer rest with individuals.

Bailout of Delinquent Homeowners

Obama Administration officials and various state Attorneys General looked gleeful in January 2012 announcing a $25 billion settlement with five big banks—and why not? The bankers coughed up shareholder money to settle a pseudo-foreclosure scandal, while the White House moved closer to its political goal of guaranteeing every home mortgage.

Rarely have so many politicians cashed in so blatantly on so little wrong-doing. In 2010, a group of State Attorneys General led by Iowa's Tom Miller spotted political gold in reports that some bank employees had approved legal mortgage loan documents without proper review. They quickly spun this into the fairy tale that evil banks were kicking borrowers out of their homes for no good reason. Former Ohio Attorney General Richard Cordray, who parlayed his scare campaign into a job running the new Consumer Financial Protection Bureau, said banks had "a business model based on fraud," (A very blatant, but convenient government lie).

The banks did have sloppy paperwork practices, but they were also dealing with a gargantuan, historic wave of foreclosures created in large part by government-backed Fannie Mae and Freddie Mac stupidity.

But the politicians know an election-year windfall when they see it. Ally Financial, Bank of America, Citigroup, J.P. Morgan Chase and Wells Fargo promised to devote a mere $1.5 billion of the $25 billion to alleged victims of wrongful foreclosures between January 1, 2008 and December 31, 2011.

The rest of the loot will serve the political agenda of paying off favored homeowners—meaning voters—with principal reductions, refinancing programs and foreclosure forbearance. The states and feds will also get nice cash payments. Think of this as one more giant political stimulus package— Congressional approval not required.

At least $10 billion will go toward principal reduction for delinquent borrowers or those on the brink of foreclosure with loans issued by private lenders. In other words, Washington is taking money from bank shareholders and investors in mortgage-backed securities, who will see the value of their holdings fall, and giving it to people who aren't paying their mortgages, thereby being rewarded for not doing so.

Incredibly, the settlement doesn't prevent states or the feds from pursuing more criminal cases, civil-rights or securitization lawsuits. So even after this round of political extortion, the banks will be asked to pay again and again. They have little ability to say no because Mr. Cordray and regulators now have life-or-death control over nearly every bank product.

In reality however, the affected banks could not be happier could they? Through the government's largesse, they (being only a "select few" of all banks or other holders of delinquent mortgages) will receive a huge pay-down on non-performing assets (at taxpayer expense) and have to come up with barely a smidgeon of the "cost." And the favor is easily returned and the political favoritism can easily be continued and enlarged by making strategic campaign donations, with the very funds that were provided by the taxpayers. So everyone wins, right? The banks get what they want, politicians are made out to be "helping," and the unfortunate homeowners get a reprieve thanks to their ever-loving government, the economy is helped out resulting in more jobs, and banks will now have more funds with which to loan.

All of this will entrench the government ever-deeper into the housing market, and this may be the real political goal anyway. In January 2012 the Administration announced it would take billions of dollars in leftover TARP funds to entice Fannie and Freddie's regulator to do principal write-downs. In that month the White House asked Congress to let the taxpayer-backed Federal Housing Administration—which is already insolvent—underwrite loan refinancing for underwater borrowers with private mortgages. What this means is a further shifting of mortgage risk to the Federal Government instead of where it belongs, with individuals and their free-market lenders.

President Obama explains the details of the settlement.

Obama added, when announcing this new give-away program, that he hopes "widespread" principal reductions become "commonplace" and he also said, "We're going to keep on at it until everyone shares in America's comeback." Translation: The politicized lending that led to the housing crisis has turned into politicized settlements, which will in turn lead to more politicized lending.

However this helps the politicians, it won't revive the housing market. CoreLogic's latest data show some 10.7 million residential properties have underwater mortgages, representing 22.1% of all housing loans, or $699 billion. Even $25 billion in income redistribution can't clear the market any faster of excess homes, or produce more buyers who can afford to buy them. Presumably that can wait for the second Obama term.

And the list goes on and on and on. The propaganda machine is working overtime. Banks, businesses, individuals, and state governments continue feeding at the public trough with reckless abandon.

How are all these Entitlement Programs Being Paid For?

Before Wilson, Hoover and FDR, entitlement programs were largely paid for from tax revenues. And whenever the government went into debt, there was considerable pressure to get back out of debt and balance the budget. But during the depression when these programs were greatly enlarged and especially to finance the WWII war effort, the Government incurred huge deficits and borrowed money by selling bonds to individuals, business entities, investors, countries and so on.

Since then the National Debt has become the weapon of choice to provide the funds needed to meet the exponential growth of entitlement programs.

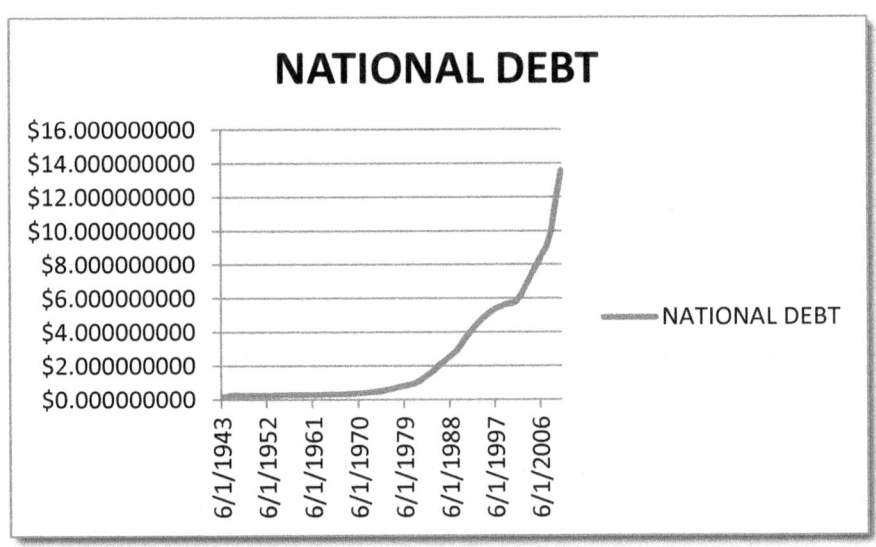

The National Debt has risen from $0.77 Trillion to almost $16.0 Trillion in less than 30 years, an increase of over 2,000 per cent.

To gain a bit better perspective, consider the following illustration comparing two periods of National Debt growth:

The Pursuit of Happiness

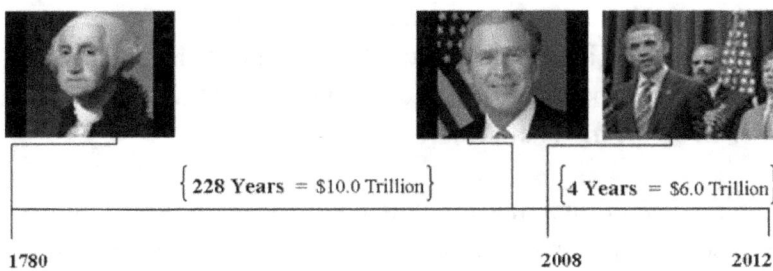

| { 228 Years = $10.0 Trillion } | { 4 Years = $6.0 Trillion } |

1780   2008   2012

In 228 years the National Debt grew $10.0 Trillion, and in not yet 4 years of the Obama Administration, it grew by $6.0 Trillion. (All figures in constant 2008 dollars)

Here is a pie chart of the US Government total spending level in fiscal 2011:

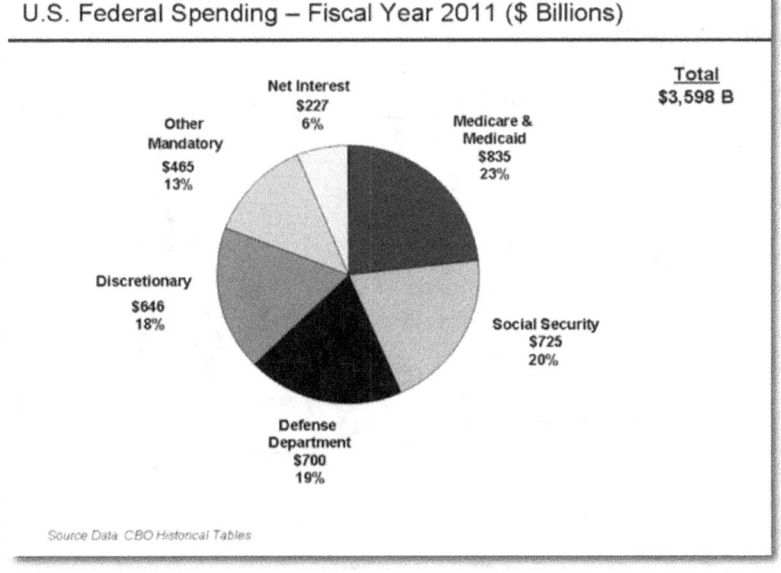

U.S. Federal Spending – Fiscal Year 2011 ($ Billions)

Tax receipts for the same period were $2,303 Billion resulting in a $1.3 Trillion shortfall added to the National Debt in only one year. That represents spending of almost 40% more than revenues taken in. A full 63% of all government spending is for mandatory expenditures; in other words, entitlements plus interest on the national debt.

There is simply no way that this trend can be reversed and is precisely why the governmental OMB department says that entitlement programs are unsustainable. The proclivity to entitlement spending financed by debt growth is now so overwhelming that there is not even a whisper of a notion of the national debt ever being paid back, nor of there ever being a successful movement to balance the US budget; as to do so would leave next to nothing left over for discretionary spending.

Still not convinced this nation is in financial trouble? Then be prepared to digest the following:

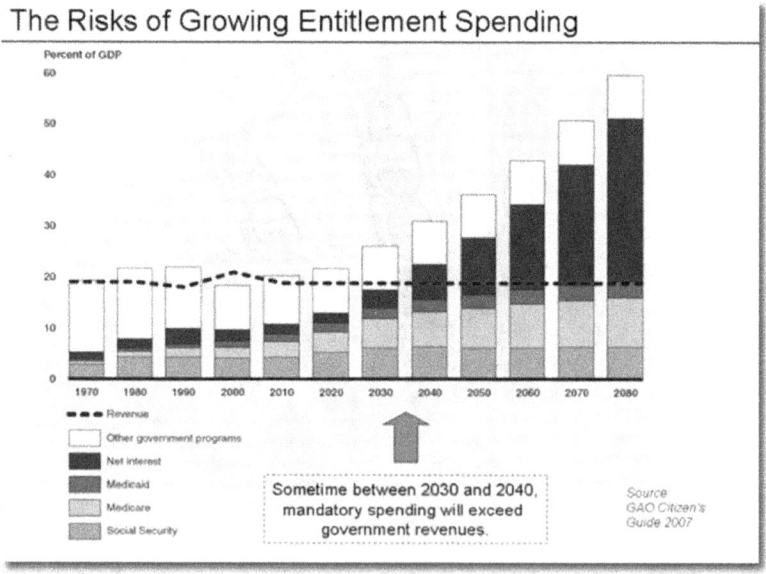

Interest on the National Debt (in red) alone will be enough to bury us, but entitlement programs will complete the job much sooner, probably within 20 years or less from now. Why is that? Because we have barely touched on the section entitled "Other Government Programs"; such as the Business and Bank Bailouts, not to mention bailouts that will be needed to rescue many of the existing 34 "bankrupt" States that are clearly themselves under water. And what if European (EU) Countries currently floundering in their own entitlement budgetary morasses need bailing out? They will turn to the world's "Bank of Last Resort," the US Federal Reserve which is currently keeping them afloat via the World Bank and the IMF.

What can be done?
The US Government has three choices; 1) raise tax revenues, 2) cut entitlements, or 3) deficit spend---that's it. Currently, with almost 50% of all eligible taxpayers paying zero taxes, that leaves middle-income earners and the wealthy from which to extract more money. But guess what? To meet the required expenditures in as soon as 2025, taxing these people to the tune of 100% of all their incomes will not be enough to cover outlays. Obviously, higher taxes are not the answer.

Cutting entitlements, are you kidding? Just take a look at what's happening in Greece, Italy, Spain and elsewhere, when austerity plans (translation: cutting benefits) is merely threatened...there is violent rioting in the streets. That will happen here too. No, cutting entitlement benefits will be devastating because this nation is hooked on entitlements.

Deficit spending is the only answer left and seems to be the method of choice. And the deleterious effects are not immediately felt or made obvious. So what if the curves and graphs show almost vertical growth lines? Who cares?

In time, everyone will. Rest assured those harmful effects will be felt soon enough, when hyper-inflation raises its ugly head and spirals out of control. That has always been what brings Socialism to its knees and has destroyed all such societies in the past.

CHAPTER 10

─────◉─────

INFLATION - THE HIDDEN TAX

To most Americans inflation is rising prices. Americans have been conditioned to believe rising prices are inevitable, a fact of life. "Face it Dad, those days are ancient...you're just getting old," my kids loved to say. "Get used to it, these are modern times."

Prices increase for a number of reasons, one being from an increase in demand as we have recently seen which caused the meteoric rise in real estate values. Economists refer to this as Demand Pull inflation. Another, known as Cost Push inflation occurs, for example, when a natural resource becomes depleted or increasingly rare and costs more to find or develop.

But true inflation can be most easily described by saying...Inflation results when too many dollars are chasing too few goods. That's a condition that has nothing to do with Cost Push or Demand Pull because it relates to the country's money supply.

Remember that money is a commodity and its value is determined or influenced by the law of supply and demand. Properly regulated, to be increased when productivity demands more of it and decreased when inflation demands it, money will remain stable, and reliably constant. When the supply of money is increased beyond what is needed to service the needs of productivity, its value plummets. That is bad and this example will illustrate why.

Say you have two people or entities and one wants to purchase a home and can't pay cash for it. The other lends money for it

163

and agrees to a 30-year payback. If during that period the value of the money is seriously diminished, the borrower benefits because he is paying back the loan with less valuable more plentiful dollars and the lender ends up with less value in return, for the same reason.

In America, the task of maintaining a consistent value of the US Dollar supposedly rests with the Federal Reserve System. And through its "Open Window" process it does this by buying or selling US Bonds and by regulating the interest rates banks charge each other. These two processes are supposed to regulate the supply of money in the economy. However, the value of the US dollar is felt throughout the world because the dollar is currently the world's reserve currency, the benchmark upon which all other world currencies are traded. The dollar has become the benchmark, because all countries have discontinued using gold as the backing for their currencies, temporarily that is, and the dollar is recognized as the most "stable" of all other currencies.

Enter the US Government, via the US Treasury Department, which is tasked with providing the cash needed to cover the Government's total expenditures. When tax revenues fall short, the Treasury Department orders the Fed (the Federal Reserve Bank) to print up more US Bonds plus the needed paperbacks. The Government takes the cash and the bonds are given to the Fed. The cash is then put into circulation with total disregard as to its effect on the supply of money. Total disregard because that process is based on political decisions and not based on monetary policy. That's why Keynesian economics is proven to be bankrupt because these decisions are politicized and are not driven by their effect on the economy.

Pumping vast amounts of money into the economy, above and beyond that which is needed to support productivity, does nothing to promote economic prosperity. In fact, it does just the opposite. It lowers the value of the Nation's currency and robs people of their wealth, their property, and their standard of living, without them even knowing it. It is...the ultimate form of taxation, the hidden tax.

All Socialistic governments have employed this method to deliver their notions of benefits to the people and have systematically destroyed their monetary systems in the process. US politicians love to speak of the necessity of more regulation of American banks, and accuse businesses and the wealthy (who "don't pay their fair share") as the "culprits" responsible for the destruction of American prosperity, when in fact they (the politicians) are the ones most responsible for that destruction.

The US Treasury and the Federal Reserve are pouring dollars into the economy far and above that which will stabilize and sustain the value of the currency and will continue to do so because entitlement demands will blow the roof off in a very short period of time.

Oh yes, currently the US Bond market seems to be shakily stable, but that is only because the value of European Government debt is plummeting and US debt is considered the best of the worst as far as investors are concerned. That will change, soon enough.

The world will be awash with worthless greenbacks, the US dollar will cease to be the world's reserve currency and gold will once again be restored to its predominance as the true currency reserve—until, that is, the next cataclysmic round of Socialism. China, currently buying up the world's supply of gold (and is also the world's biggest gold producer) will soon become the predominant economic force in the world, and the

Renminbi will probably become the world's next reserve currency. And do the Chinese know anything about Socialism? Evidently not enough, not yet anyway.

Socialism dampens the entrepreneurial spirit upon which this Nation was founded. It chokes the engines of prosperity; it destroys freedom and takes liberty from those the Constitution was designed to protect. The rights of property are dismantled and trampled upon, mutilated and even disdained, by a society drunken with the entitlement mentality. And inflation finishes the job of social destruction through devaluation of currencies.

A correction is soon to be implemented. Can this Nation endure? Can the principles of freedom be wrested from the wreckage and carnage? Will this nation be taken over by a dictator like all others in the past? Can the ship be righted?

I believe it can. I believe it will. Regardless of how popular and powerful politicians might strive to become, I believe Americans are still more inclined to more greatly cherish freedom and the republic instead of oligarchy. I have faith in the righteous principles upon which this nation was built, and I believe there are enough people who not only know about these principles but cherish and live them, believe in them and will fight for them.

Will you help? Will you stand forth? Can you articulate them well enough? Can you live them? Do you want to win? Then wake up and move it!

SECTION THREE
THE PURSUIT OF HAPPINESS

"Men are that they might have joy"

Does life really begin at 40?

There are many clichés, words of wisdom and philosophies whereby the ideas of happiness are meant to be discovered or defined. Some are true and helpful while others are not. They work for some but not others. In the end, perhaps, Will Rogers had it right when he said, "Life is what you make it." So, is happiness natural and spontaneous, or is it a figment of the imagination, contrived and manufactured only with effort?

Probably, it is a little of both. But one thing is certain. The pursuit of happiness is perhaps the most universal of all endeavors of mankind, after the will to live. The will to live, thrive and be happy is instinctive, bred into man from the beginning--even before mortality began.

Our Pre-Earthly Existence and
the Purpose of Life

Liberty and man's Free Agency were in existence in the pre-earthly sphere of life. They were, however, hotly debated by the children of God. At the root of the debate lay the real purpose of our future earthly life. God meant it when he said, "Men are that they might have joy."

As children of Heavenly Father (Heavenly Parents, really) our joy and happiness was not complete nor could it ever be by remaining in that sphere. All that God is and/or has in store for His children could not be obtained or achieved without a mortal existence, whereby we could gain a physical body and be tested (i.e. learn to be like Him outside His presence). The combination of these and many other things and by being obedient to correct principles would in the end provide the means of our achieving all the joy and happiness that God enjoys. God promised us all that He has, conditionally.

In that pre-mortal existence, the debate raged over whether all or just some of His children could obtain or inherit this joy and happiness. On the one side, was the contention that no one should be lost and that every soul should not go without it (i.e. equal result). That seemed to be the epitome of compassion and fairness. No one should have more or less than another. All should be winners. There should be no losers. On the face, it was (and continues to be here on earth) a powerful argument and was enough to convince many to not only believe it but to demand it. Those that did, "kept not their first estate" and were denied the opportunity to advance into mortality, and were cast out.

The problem with that side of the debate was that in order to achieve universal success and equity, it would require the elimination of freedom of choice…mans' agency. And that was its downfall. It flew in the face of natural law, God's law. It would defeat the very purpose of earth life and the eternal pursuit of true happiness and joy, because those virtues can only be achieved willingly and voluntarily, by exercise of free choice and by obedience to correct principles.

CHAPTER 1

———————●———————

FORCED COMPASSION IS NOT COMPASSION AT ALL

Let's first talk about what happiness is not. To accomplish the ends of Socialism, it requires extensive use of propaganda centering on the appeal to people's compassion and notions of fairness. It is the driving force which impels societies to accept Socialism in the first place. Never mind that to put it into play requires the strong arm of the law, police force. That is carefully concealed or ignored, and besides, the people who have what others don't have are painted as not deserving, selfish, or not caring at all. Compassion and caring are the clarion calls to greater socialism. It is a slippery slope and once society is hooked, it is not likely to realize it has embarked onto the highway to slavery.

But why speak of slavery when all that is wanted is everyone to be happy and to have what everyone else has? What is so wrong with that, huh?

Nothing...except that it is a counterfeit notion. It flies in the face of reality. No one is equal. We are as different from one another as there are different fingerprints or DNA markers. Some prefer roses while others like daisies. Some want large families while others prefer none, and so on. You make the list, but set aside many hours because your list will be endless.

Putting people into chains to satisfy someone's notions of equality and fairness can never be considered a source of happiness neither for the one's being extorted nor the ones on the dole. Slavery works to engulf both. It dampens and destroys the will and incentive to produce on both sides; the giver as well as the receiver. It mocks the universal spirit of choice and freedom eventually eliminating them altogether, until society is in the refrigerator; "the door is closed, the lights are out, the eggs are coolin', the jello is jigglin', and the butter is gettin' hard" as Chick Hearn would say. Except there are no winners in that game, only losers. Totalitarianism has taken over. The dictators are in place and those in jail are plotting the next coup d'etat until the next dictator comes forth to save the day. Thus history repeats itself.

It is hard not to conclude that underlying it all there is a conspiracy. What else could drive these seemingly mindless politicians onward? Don't they know what they are doing? Why would they drive society into more dependence on central governments? Why do they say what people want to hear and then do the opposite once in power?

Because Socialism is founded upon lie after lie. The end justifies the means and it doesn't matter how Socialism wins; just that it does.

The Evils of the Dole
Forced compassion is counterfeit. Anything too easily obtained is of no value at all nor is it appreciated. This is a true principle. So is the opposite, that when one works for what he gets one appreciates and cherishes it all the more. And since satisfaction comes not from receiving what one does not sacrifice for, one is seldom if ever satisfied the more he so receives. That is the evil of the dole. The dole also makes masters of the giver (the government) and slaves of the receivers. How can that be considered happiness? Does anyone really believe that when

the light of day is shed upon it? Socialism is nothing more than a recipe for misery and breeds malcontent.

Socialist governments including the American form of social welfare, more than anything else, have brought misery and destruction to the family unit, destroyed the incentive to work and produce, reduced the economic well-being, and yes even the spiritual well-being of its subjects and citizens than perhaps any other evil force in the world.

Work is meant to be enthroned

When Adam and Eve were cast out of the garden, the Lord pronounced this edict: "By the sweat of thy face shalt thou eat all the days of thy life." To many this is considered punishment sent down by God because of Adam's transgression. It was, in fact, a blessing in disguise. And to make sure mankind would get the point, God said that thistles, thorns and noxious weeds would torment man along the way. In other words, it was not meant to be easy. Anything easily obtained is never fully appreciated. Without opposition man could never know and appreciate what was good.

The dole destroys industry and thrift, just as work builds satisfaction and contentment. Things that are obtained from work even with adversity being strewn along the way, are more highly regarded and cherished. No one knows this better than one who has walked the path. Recognizing this fact does more to bring happiness on this earth than perhaps anything else. It is not in what one has necessarily, but in the process of achieving it that brings peace, contentment and happiness.

The Pursuit of Happiness

CHAPTER 2

========◉========

AMERICA'S FREEDOMS ALLOW THE PURSUIT OF HAPPINESS

Americans already have more than anyone else

No nation on earth eats as well as our nation. No country is so well clothed. No people are so well housed. No individuals on this earth have so many of the conveniences as we do in terms of heating, air conditioning, lighting, plumbing, and other comforts. These are not luxuries enjoyed by the rich alone; these are the comforts of the common people, comforts enjoyed by even the poorest among us, comforts of which even mighty monarchs of the past only dreamed.

Few nations enjoy the freedoms we have—the freedom to speak, freedom to own property and businesses or to participate in ownership, freedom to worship, freedom to print, freedom to travel at home and abroad, freedom to censure even public officials, and freedom to have the privacy we desire.

No country has been more concerned with due process in its judicial system than ours. The protection of human rights, as granted by our Constitution and Bill of Rights, is not just theory. And no nation has done more to extend these very blessings to other nations and peoples and to have done so without conquering other nations to be absorbed into our empire.

No other country has been so generous as America in terms of its money and food. No other nation has fought starvation and economic collapse, tyranny and oppression, and come to the rescue of nations struck by natural disaster as America has.

And most if not all these things we have as Americans have been achieved not by government nor from governmental coercion but from the people exercising their rights as a free people through their industry and thrift. And in part, that's what it means to be an American, to enjoy the freedoms we have which have allowed us to propel ourselves to the level of our successes and to allow people to pursue whatever makes them happy.

CHAPTER 3

IF YE KEEP MY COMMANDMENTS, YE SHALL PROSPER

There are many in this country who believe this is a land choice above all other lands and that it is granted to a choice, God-fearing people who wish to follow His teachings and commandments and shall remain here on this land as we remain in God's divine favor. There are principles which, if applied and acted upon, are conducive to the social, spiritual, and economic well-being of the Nation. They are basic to sound international as well as domestic tranquility. They are designed to plumb the depths of human motives and urges and to govern the baser parts of man's nature.

They came from God Himself and form the foundation for an enduring, civilized society, any society. And they are embodied in the Ten Commandments. No nation whose majority of people who have kept these commandments has ever perished. However, there have been many whose majority of peoples who have violated these principles have perished as whole societies. That list is long.

These commandments, known as the Decalogue, begin first with a stipulation of the sovereignty of God providing for our allegiance to Him. This is followed by the declaration of treason against Him with its requisite punishment. Then follows the law against blasphemy; declaring that those who blaspheme will not be held guiltless. These first three commandments circumscribe man's relationships with the Almighty.

The balance of the Decalogue deals with man's relationships with his fellowman. In them is the promulgation of law governing family relationships, parent and child; the law that specifies periods of work and rest, the relationship of capital and labor; the principles that govern civic relationships and declare social order—the 'Thou shalt nots.'

In these Ten Commandments, the basis for sound civil society is founded allowing it to grow and flourish. When a majority of peoples violate or forget these principles the society deteriorates and degenerates; greed, unbridled passion and pride, jealousy and hatred, fear and mistrust, and dependency on overlords rather than on God, overcome those who will to do good. Wars emerge, the society implodes, and a new society is born. But unless its replacement is again founded upon these sound principles the replacements remain unstable. Often righteous-loving peoples have had to leave and migrate to new lands, establishing new societies based on these proven and sound principles, such as the one on which we now live—the American Continent.

God had a hand in preserving this land for just such a migration; a hand in leading, guiding and drawing righteous-loving people from all other lands; a hand in establishing a Constitution founded on compatible principles to His great commandments; a hand in allowing its citizens to pursue happiness unencumbered from tyranny, force and oppression. The resulting society exudes testimony of the truthfulness of this chapter's heading. That title is a direct quote, a promise from the Almighty Himself; "If ye keep my commandments, ye shall prosper in the land."

Jesus, when asked by his detractors, "Master which is the Greatest Commandment?" responded with one they had never heard of—"Thou Shalt Love the Lord thy God with all thy might, mind and strength." In other times alone with His followers, He expanded on that with "If ye love me, keep my commandments." He and God have both said that the words of this chapter's heading prescribe what happens to those who follow this great teaching.

Love God, love righteous principles, and happiness and prosperity follow those who do. Love of God, love of sound righteous principles is the foundation for happiness in this life as well as that of the next. Let there be no mistake. Anything less can never bring lasting happiness.

The Pursuit of Happiness

CHAPTER 4

————●————

IMPORTANCE OF
THE NUCLEAR FAMILY

Ponder for a moment this great commandment—"Honor thy father and thy mother." Almost all animals on earth do not mate for life. Their primary objective is survival and their days are filled with foraging for food and being on the lookout for their safety. Along the way, instinct drives them to procreate and build temporary nests. Habit and instinct are their highest form of achievement. They either abandon their offspring upon initial inception or shortly thereafter, remaining together for only a very short period of time.

In contrast, humans by way of reason, analysis, intelligence and quest for achievement are closer to that God which gives them existence. They are capable of reaching for the stars, finding peace and solace with their mates, and feeling close to their maker. They show love and concern for one another by binding together through commitment and devotion. The act of procreation exists in the highest form of physical and emotional expression. Trust and honesty cements their solidarity. Gestation periods are long and development to maturity even longer. Families made up of fathers and mothers who nurture and care for their young, and not only for their food, clothing and housing needs but for their full needs and requirements launch them into life where they can soar to whatever heights they are capable of. All of this takes sacrifice, commitment, solidarity, love and devotion.

But families don't terminate when children leave the roost. God intended for families (His children, really) to be knit together throughout eternity. That thread of connection is held together when children continue to honor, connect, love and in turn care for their parents until their departure from this world.

The commandment to honor parents was not accompanied by conditions, that one only need to obey, if parents were or did something. All parents deserve to be honored in some way no matter what. Loving thy neighbor as thyself includes thy parents first and foremost.

If nothing more in this life is learned than the fact that life is hard, that it requires effort, and constant attention, then mortality has taught us well. Everyone knows that success in any venture is fraught with risk, requires effort and perseverance, and that the things achieved are most cherished after putting in the necessary effort. This is true in all aspects of life and especially in familial pursuits.

Can one be happy raised in a one parent or a non-nuclear family of any sort? Of course. But joy and happiness is reached at its fullest extent possible when one is raised in a solid two-parent family consisting of a father and mother, founded upon honest, trustworthy commitments, and nurtured in principles designed to lift and exalt. There is no greater benefit that can come to human beings than what is prescribed by the Almighty with respect to families so structured.

Commitment, dedication and love bond the family unit. If parents only exist to provide physical safety, nourishment, clothing and shelter and their children are awash in pleasure and entertainment they will fail in their duty. Parents need to convey the higher forms of living; that of social congeniality, emotional maturity, spiritual reverence and moral obligation, civic duty; the need, desire, objective, and rewards of service to others, and be the example of all these traits. Along the way, children need to understand and know what it means to be an

American; what is meant by freedom and liberty; how free enterprise unfettered by governmental restrictions and greed of the unworthy provides the greatest opportunity for prosperity and advancement; how education and hard work through overcoming risk and through perseverance not only provide for earthly needs but the supreme satisfaction in their accomplishment.

Sadly, more and more of these types of families are disappearing from the landscape and America is suffering because of it. Alternate lifestyles, adoration of pleasure and useless pastimes, broken families, lack of commitment in conjugal and marital relations, the debasement of sex and the human body, disdain towards the successful, disrespect for authority, mindless trampling of the rights of others especially the weak and unborn, loss of spiritual connection to the Almighty, and the rise in the notion that truth and obedience to law is relative rather than absolute; all these are destructive forces and if they envelope the majority of its peoples, this nation will not, cannot endure as we have known it.

Our only hope is in the preponderance, perseverance and endurance of strong, nuclear families.

The Pursuit of Happiness

CHAPTER 5

ENTHRONEMENT OF WORK

As a boy growing up whenever my father or mother spoke of "work," that meant misery to me. Being in the hot sun or icy cold, pulling weeds, mowing the lawn, or shoveling snow meant less time spent with friends or playing with whatever, not to mention the pain and suffering that work always brought. We lived on a fairly large lot, 90 by 200 feet, with about half that in a garden and a chicken coop. During summers my father insisted on my getting jobs with the local farmers stacking hay, picking corn, thinning and hoeing sugar beets, cleaning chicken coops, shoveling corn silage, and building fences. Working the garden, I thought, was a giant waste of time because compared to the low cost of fresh fruits and vegetables from the market, it seemed more costly to raise your own. But my parents had lived through the Great Depression as a young married couple with small children and had learned the great values of hard work. Although they provided for my clothes and other necessities, I never received an allowance for spending money. Instead, I worked for it. I'm glad they instilled in me not only the need for hard work, but eventually the joy of it too.

I was always glad to observe the accomplishments and results of my hard work and grew to be proud of what I achieved; not to mention the cash that it put into my wallet which I was wont to spend wisely because it was so hard to replace.

The Lord said men would have to survive by the sweat of their brow; a blessing in disguise. Setbacks and challenges, overcome by hard work, bring untold blessings; the receipt of which inevitably bring with them great satisfaction and yes even joy.

183

An age old saying is Necessity is the Mother of Invention, and invention increases efficiency and productivity. The industrial revolution proves how that works. That is well and good, but at the core of all is this most important fact: that work itself brings joy and happiness.

At the height of the Depression, when unemployment was over 20% and men and women formed long lines to get soup, and they turned to government for more and more help, certain Christians were advised by wise leaders with this instruction.

"The aim of the Church is to help the people help themselves. Work is to be re-enthroned as the ruling principle in our lives."

Individual industry and thrift were re-discovered in America in the Plymouth Colony after an experiment with socialism was tried which brought the Colony to the brink of famine and extinction. Governor Bradford, with the approval of certain chief men of the colony, set aside the hollow notion that the most able and fit expended their strength and industry to support other men's wives and children. They rejected the forced compassion for others, a kind of slavery that had proven to be unproductive, a failure and what they deemed to be repugnant. Bradford then assigned to every family a parcel of land according to the proportion of their number. "This," he said, "had very good success; for it made all hands very industrious, so as much more corn was planted than otherwise would have been...The women now went willingly into the field, and took their little ones with them to set corn, which before would allege weakness, and inabilities; whom to have compelled would have been thought great tyranny and oppression." (William T. David, ed., Bradford's History of Plantation, 1606-1646, 1908, pp. 146f.).

America has enjoyed the highest productivity per capita in the world for many years and consequently the highest per capita prosperity. Upon that fact alone, right now, rests the strength of the whole world until it too will probably become overburdened and unable to support the growing apathetic entitlement mentality crushing world productivity. Right now, at the brink, is when America has to re-hear that sage advice that work should be re-enthroned.

A Simple Formula

The principles behind this original American philosophy can be reduced to a rather simple formula:

1. Economic security for all is impossible without abundance.
2. Abundance is impossible without industrious and efficient production.
3. Such production is impossible without energetic, willing, and eager labor.
4. This is not possible without incentive.
5. Of all forms of incentive, the freedom to attain a reward for one's labor is the most sustaining for most people. Sometimes called the profit motive, it is simply the right to plan and to earn and to enjoy the fruits of one's labor.

The notion that we appreciate more what is hard to come by is not an empty one. We enjoy the fruits of our labor. What is that if not happiness? Work brings happiness and that is the truth.

The sum total of all work of the whole population is referred to as the economy. What type of economy provides for the most happiness possible for the most people, is a question posed so often. The best answer is that of a free market allowing open competition. In a free market everyone has a chance to cast his vote in the election that will decide what is a fair price, a fair wage, and a fair profit; what should be produced and in what quantities and at the least cost.

All agree that the democratic process and the free market—both parts of our American way of life—are not perfect, but they are believed to have fewer faults and do a better job and provide the most happiness than any other system known to mankind.

CHAPTER 6

————— ● —————

HAPPINESS IS A PURSUIT

In all things, God wants his children to be happy. Jesus said:

"I came into the world that they might have life, and that they might have it more abundantly."

The very purpose of this life is to prepare for and become deserving of eternal happiness which God has prepared for us. And in the course leading to that end, in other words in this mortal life, God has also said that happiness is meant to be ours as well, indeed the act of preparing for that promised eternal happiness results in happiness per se.

God has also indicated that all things which come of the earth, in the season thereof, are made for the benefit and the use of man, both to please the eye and to gladden the heart. Yes even for food and for raiment, for taste and for smell, to strengthen the body and to enliven the soul. And it pleases God that He has given all these things unto man for man's benefit and happiness and He intends that they are to be used with judgment, not to excess or waste, nor to be used by extortion.

Happiness is a Choice

God has granted us the right of agency, choice. That alone is the basis for happiness for without it we would know neither joy nor misery. Even the Evil One knows that without agency we could neither know or experience good or evil, pleasure or pain, virtue or vice, love or hate, joy or misery.

187

Along with that agency, God has granted everyone the knowledge of good and evil that one can thereby make proper choices if one listens to their inner promptings. That spirit is made available to all and if heeded, one can navigate life towards the happiness God intends for all His children.

These truths apply to all men no matter their station or circumstance. There are no exceptions, no conditions upon which these laws of life are found inviolate or illusory where a person has any capability of reason or awareness. And so making proper choices leads to happiness for happiness is the natural outcome of proper choices. It is the natural order of things which God has designed for man and if only man can have faith in God that this is so, that proper choices lead to happiness, he will then come to know of its surety. And therein lies the test of our mortal existence.

If we are not really the children of our Heavenly Father, who placed us here by design and for a purpose, and if there were not absolute spiritual as well as physical laws that we violate at our peril, then man has to be appealed to on different grounds, and that is a task that is next to impossible. For if we are merely transients in an unexplainable world, we will act more as tourists than residents!

Wickedness Never Was Happiness
An ancient prophet, in advising his son who was involved sexually with a promiscuous woman, gave this sage advice, that "Wickedness never was happiness." Hedonistic pleasure-seeking offers temporary satisfaction but does not lead to more rewarding happiness or joy. Physical intimacies of indiscriminant, random, and varied connections are not inherently manifestations of the higher virtues of life; that of love, commitment, trust, and common union. The violation of these higher virtues is the wickedness the prophet was referring

to. Physical pleasures without depth are being paraded as the real thing when in fact they are not, but merely counterfeit instead. Freedom from moral or social restraints makes individuals very unhappy in the long run.

What Happiness is - A Beginning

Here are the things that form basic happiness: Personal freedoms, love and marriage, a belief in God, friendships, work, achievement, volunteering or service to others, and charitable giving. All these things are inherently "righteous." God wants us to have agency, to be and stay married, to worship and give thanks to Him, to love our neighbors as ourselves, to work, to serve others and to give of our substance to the poor and misfortunate. Together all these things form the basis for earthly happiness. There is more to happiness, of course, but these are a great foundational beginning.

The Pursuit of Happiness

CHAPTER 7

━━━●━━━

LOVE, MARRIAGE AND THE VALUE OF COMMITMENT

Men and Women are Equal in the Eyes of God

Women down through the ages, in many cultures and countries, even right up to this very age, have been and still are treated as mere chattel. They are not considered equal to men but exist to serve men in all aspects of life. They have been degraded, humiliated, treated with contempt, stripped of their God-given rights, given second-class citizenship, and in countless ways deprived of equality that is their right as daughters of God.

The age of enlightenment has not penetrated the darkness (that of the treatment of women) that still exists in the world today. Countries, cultures, societies and religions right now, even today, put women in servitude and bondage and deprive them the rights and dignity granted to men and even boys. This is a moral tragedy beyond any other, affecting countless millions of helpless women. God cannot be pleased in this, and many will be held accountable for this travesty.

God loves all his children both men and women. Both are vital to God's plan for happiness. Each has his or her vital roles and one is no more important than the other. God has never indicated otherwise. At least the Judeo-Christian God, the true God hasn't.

The Need to Feel Cherished

All men and women have basic needs and one of them seems to be that everyone wants to be cherished by someone, no matter what. Kind and loving parents fulfill this vital function to children, the more the better. And conversely, less leaves

191

children worse off. Love, acceptance, mutual trust, contentment, commitment and more, seal human bonding.

Scripture tells us that God loves every one of His children, unconditionally. Even when we disobey, He will never give up on us and if we repent He will forgive, always. Parents, by example, can more readily teach children this valuable concept, so that even if in life others fail us, we can know that our parents and God will never forsake us.

Nevertheless, human beings still need the peace and satisfaction that there is at least one person, more than anyone else, who loves and cherishes us....no matter what, through thick, thin and everything in-between. It is a cold and dreary existence when one is forced to navigate life entirely alone. "No man is an island," that's for sure.

God's intention for mortal life is for all his children to be able to come to this earth in pursuit of the eternal progress He has planned for us. We only get here by conception and birth...there is no other way. At least that is the natural way. And God has wisely prescribed that supreme human bonding is best accomplished beginning when children are born into families, complete with a father, a mother, grandparents and so on, and the family is bonded together with acceptance, love, trust and supreme solidarity. There is no better way known to man in his pursuit towards supreme happiness.

So called alternate life styles can fulfill some of human bonding needs but can never even come close to the potential made available to man through the nuclear family unit. For one thing, and a very significant one at that, is the joyful and rewarding experience of procreation from beginning to end. The physical union of intimate sexual relations; the metaphysical connection (transcending the physical and material); the very godlike ability to create life together through giving birth and life to another; all provide an almost inexplicable source of happiness and joy that cannot be matched in any other way.

This phenomenon is clearly meant as a blessing from God. It is a sacred one, meant by God to be treated as such. This because of how God views the value of each and every life. The process, right, and duty of procreation should not be violated in any way; held in contempt or treated lightly, degraded or made vile through promiscuity and love of pleasure, passion or greed, or through lack of commitment.

In this way, man can best find fulfillment of the need first spoken of in this chapter that of the need to feel cherished.

The act of physical intimacy between an unmarried man and a woman is the one most violated by man in the degradation of the nuclear family, the embodiment of God's plan for happiness. When it is based on careless passion, treated in a selfish manner, done to take advantage of another, based on a thing of the moment, or is expressed as a mere minor step above holding hands or kissing and not based on deep love and devotion, done without planning with an ultimate long-lasting goal in mind, God is unhappy. But more importantly, the act has been seriously cheapened, degraded and has become a thing of naught. There can never be true joy from that in the least. It is counterfeit in the true sense of the word.

The Value of Commitment
As children reach the age where they become aware of people outside the family unit, they look for acceptance and friendship. Playmates and siblings form bonding relationships and they begin the lifelong pursuit of finding joy in those relationships. All friendships fall into a hierarchal structure. Best friends, a person to "go steady" with, your sweetheart, one to whom you

are betrothed, and finally your life's mate; are at the top of all other relationships. In other words: best. This sticking togetherness is only established when there is an understanding of some sort of commitment between parties.

Contentment, happiness and joy spring from these lasting, bonding relationships. And commitment is the bonding agent holding every one of them together. Without commitment, humanity descends to become equal to the lowest form of animal life. There can be little fulfillment of the need to feel cherished on that level.

Commitment is outwardly defined, expressed or indicated in various ways; telling each other and everyone else, wearing a string on a finger, wearing the same item or color of clothing, wearing an engagement ring, wearing a wedding ring, signing a marriage license, saying "I Do," and so on. All these are an outward expression of commitment. And again, it is this commitment which provides the contentment, joy and happiness each one craves and needs.

We express this commitment outwardly as mentioned. These symbols and signs indicate the level of our intent. Formalizing these levels of commitment further demonstrate our meaningful intent and serve to give notice to God and the world the extent of our commitment.

In marriage, by signing the marriage contract (or license), dressing in formal, best clothing, inviting friends and family, arranging a formal or sacred setting, stating in front of God and the whole world that you will love, cherish and be committed to each other no matter what, either for eternity or until death do you part, is the ultimate form of outward commitment. And most of all, it is meant to serve notice to one another of your willingness to be so committed to the other, forsaking all others forever. There can be no higher commitment; it just doesn't exist.

Making Commitment Last

One of the earliest lessons learned in life is that all things good require effort, diligent effort. And something as important as commitment to spouse requires supreme, constant effort. "Falling in love is such a gross misnomer because being in love is not propelled downward by gravity, that is, without upward pressure. Clearly one does not fall into love but one grows into it.

But often, after the matrimonial formalities are over, one or the other, or both, take things for granted thinking that the marriage contract is sealed, the job is done, no need to worry. All the tender little things become overlooked and the high expectations begin to take over. Sometimes one has a goal of changing the other to become what one really wanted but overlooked before the marriage. The need to refresh the feelings and the expressed commitment so often shared before marriage becomes more and more vital as the marriage goes on, kids enter in, and life's challenges and adversities envelope the family.

In keeping an automobile running smoothly and serving one's needs to perfection, one needs to care for its needs; i.e. keeping fuel in the tank, fresh oil in the engine, air in the tires, and so on. And these days, the computers in the vehicles issue warnings when these needs arise. A marriage relationship also issues warnings signaling that the marriage commitment requires refreshing and replenishing.

It is foolish to ignore the need for constant refreshing the loving commitment made at the altar. Tender, loving sayings, showing heartfelt feelings, work wonders. One needs to be constantly reminded that their spouse loves them, through thick and thin. "Have I told you lately, that I love you?" is a great example. God is ever there for us. A spouse should ever be there for the other as well. Happiness will surely be yours if you follow this simple recipe. As one of my sons loves to say, "Happy wife, happy life." And he believes it and practices it every day.

CHAPTER 8

━━━●━━━

ULTIMATE HAPPINESS

In considering the full scope of mortality, it simply cannot be ignored the importance of God in our lives. Connections and commitments to one another are vital for happiness, for sure. But to ignore our relationship and need for commitments to and with God only deprives us of the greatest form of happiness that can be realized.

All believers in and worshippers of God share a common thread; they have faith in a better afterlife, believing that through their faithfulness God will reward them with ultimate happiness. That belief, that faith sustains us through thick and thin, good times and bad. That is, of course, God's intent. Even He, the greatest of all has said:

"For behold, this is my work and my glory, to bring to pass the immortality and eternal life of man." (Moses 1:39)

God intends for there to be interconnectivity between humans and himself, and not just only between him and us individually. Rather the intent is that there is to be a three-way connectivity, a tripartite arrangement involving self, spouse and others, and God, illustrated as follows:

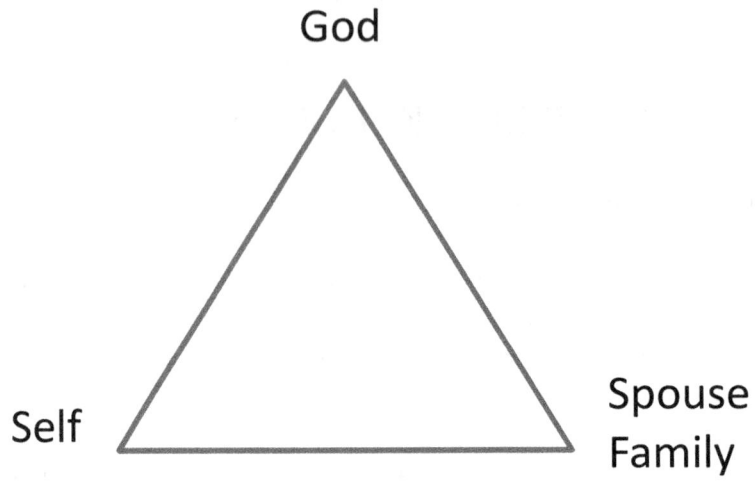

God

Self

Spouse
Family
Friends
All Others

Think of these links as partnerships complete with solemn commitments or covenants, both outward and internal, both formal and in the heart.

The interconnecting links, the glue, the transcendental bonding agents are LOVE, SERVICE, and CHARITY. Ponder this concept. Think of nothing else, just ponder it. After doing so, ask God either in your heart, with bowed head, or on your knees…if this concept is not in fact true.

Every person, no matter their station, class, era, situation, or religion, is going to be judged in the hereafter according to whatever level of God's commandments have been made known unto them. Everyone is blessed with the knowledge to know right from wrong. Supreme happiness will not only be yours in this life but especially in the one to come, if you pass that test. Everyone is accountable, no one is exempt. And Christ, through His atoning sacrifice, provides the restorative keys, after all we can do.

The Value of 'Home'

Home is a place of refuge, a foundation from which all of life springs. We go there to rest, receive nourishment and rejuvenation, to find peace, find understanding and reprieve, love and acceptance. It can be sacred or it can be hell. Members of the family, especially the parents set the tone and the example, provide the mentorship and instruction, lead and guide, nurture and protect. And almost by instinct, parents know they are charged to teach the bonding agents, LOVE, SERVICE, and CHARITY.

It is in the home where love, discipline and values are best taught and practiced. These should not be left to others such as at school, church, or most definitely not the state. No other success in life can compensate for failure in the home.

All fathers and mothers should take heed. The sin of failure in the home and in its duties falls upon the heads of parents. They are accountable. Turn off the television, control use of the Internet and games, put down the newspaper, avoid distractions, enjoy each other, and perform your duties as parents. Happiness springs from this; count on it.

The Family
Marriage between a man and a woman is ordained of God. The family is central to His plan for the eternal happiness and destiny of his children. All human beings—male and female-- are created in the image of God. Each is a beloved spirit son or daughter of heavenly parents, and as such, each has a divine nature and intended destiny. Gender is an essential characteristic of individual premortal, mortal, and eternal identity and purpose.

In the premortal realm, spirit sons and daughters knew and worshipped God as their Eternal Father and accepted His plan by which His children could obtain a physical body and gain earthly experience to progress toward perfection and ultimately realize his or her divine destiny as an heir of eternal life. The divine plan of happiness enables family relationships to be perpetuated beyond the grave. Sacred ordinances and covenants available in certain holy places make it possible for individuals to return to the presence of God and for families to be united eternally.

God's commandment for His children to multiply and replenish the earth remains in force today. God has commanded that the sacred powers of procreation are to be employed only between man and woman, lawfully wedded as husband and wife. The means by which mortal life is created is divinely appointed. God affirms the sanctity of life and its importance in His eternal plan.

Husband and wife have a solemn responsibility to love and care for each other and for their children. Parents have a sacred duty to rear their children in love and righteousness, to provide for their physical and spiritual needs, to teach them to love and serve one another to observe the commandments of God and to be law-abiding citizens where they live. Husbands and wives--- mothers and fathers---will be held accountable before God for the discharge of these duties.

The family is ordained of God. Marriage between man and woman is essential to His eternal plan. Children are entitled to birth within the bonds of matrimony, and to be reared by a father and a mother who honor marital vows with complete fidelity. Happiness in family life is most likely to be achieved when founded upon the teachings of the Lord Jesus Christ. Successful marriages and families are established and maintained on principles of faith, prayer, repentance, forgiveness, respect, love, compassion, work, and wholesome recreational activities. By divine design, fathers are to preside over their families in love and righteousness and are responsible to provide the necessities of life and protection for their families. Mothers are primarily responsible for the nurture of their children. In these sacred responsibilities, fathers and mothers are obligated to help one another as equal partners. Disability, death, or other circumstances may necessitate individual adaptation.

God warns that individuals who violate covenants of chastity, who abuse spouse or offspring, or who fail to fulfill family responsibilities will one day stand accountable before Him. God further warns that the disintegration of the family will bring upon individuals, communities, and nations the calamities foretold by ancient and modern prophets.

The family is to be protected, maintained and strengthened as the fundamental unit of society. Therein lies ultimate happiness in this life and the next.

The Pursuit of Happiness

EPILOGUE

What is sacred, divinely inspired, and of most value to man? It is in the following list:

- Life
- Liberty
- Property and the rights thereof
- Commitment to spouse, family, friends, and all others
- Forgiveness
- Obedience to righteous, moral principles
- Love, charity, and service

Know this that every soul is free,
To choose his life and what he'll be … …

And that's what it means to be an American.

www.ingramcontent.com/pod-product-compliance
Lightning Source LLC
Chambersburg PA
CBHW070004300526
45794CB00001B/174